MADE IN

MOMOYO KAIJIMA
JUNZO KURODA
YOSHIHARU TSUKAMOTO

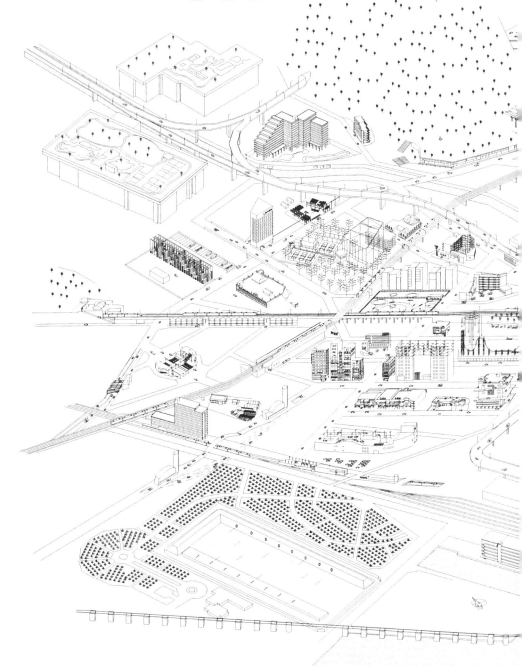

TOKYO

メイド・イン・トーキョー

貝島桃代・黒田潤三・塚本由晴

鹿島出版会

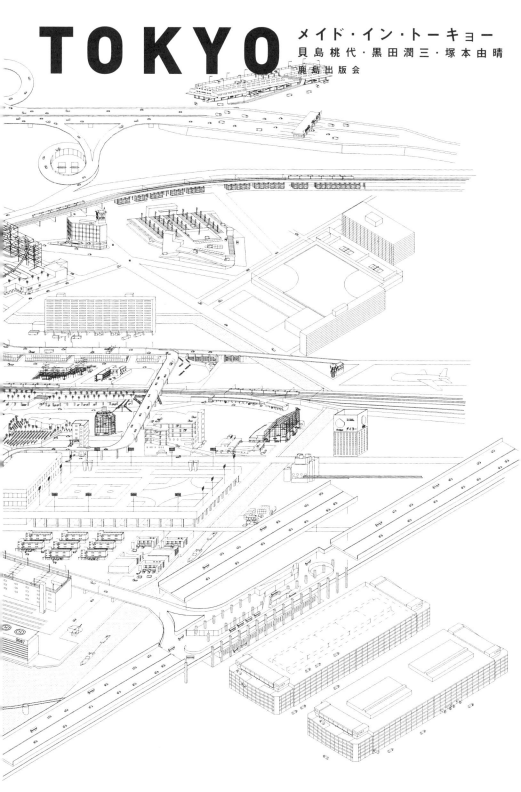

CONTENTS
目次

47 吸血公園
vampire park

48 クレーンだな
crane shelves

49 ユーレイ・ル・ファクトリー
ghost rail factory

50 擁壁マンション
retaining wall apartments

51 ブリッジハウス
bridge home

52 宅地農場
residential farm

53 物流インターチェンジ
dispersal terminal

54 ロイヤルゴルフマンション
royal golf apartments

55 カーオフィス
car parking office

56 グリーンパーキング
green parking

57 オートデパート
auto department store

58 ファミレス3兄弟
family restaurant triplets

59 青果タウン
vegetable town

60 松茸型レールビル
sprouting building

61 TRC(東京流通センター)
tokyo dispersal centre

62 冷凍団地ビル
coolroom estate

63 ペット建築1号
pet architecture 001

64 ダムマンション
dam housing

65 ジャンクションターミナル
airport junction

66 スポーツブリッジ
sports bridge

67 スポーツマン・ズー
sportsman zoo

68 ヘリ倉庫
heli-warehouse

69 洗車テラス
carwash terrace

70 射撃墓場
shooting graveyard

チーム・メイド・イン・トーキョー
TEAM MADE IN TOKYO

2001

貝島桃代 Momoyo Kaijima

黒田潤三 Junzo Kuroda

塚本由晴 Yoshiharu Tsukamoto

久野靖広 Yasuhiro Kuno

高木 俊 Shun Takagi

マリカ・ネウストプニー Marika Neustupny

nmp 2000
(Web site English version)

貝島桃代 Momoyo Kaijima

マリカ・ネウストプニー Marika Neustupny

黒田潤三 Junzo Kuroda

安野 彰 Akira Yasuno

高木 俊 Shun Takagi

塚本由晴 Yoshiharu Tsukamoto

春木裕美子 Yumiko Haruki

荻原富雄 Tomio Ogiwara

トム・ヴィンセント Tom Vincent

橘 淳子 Junko Tachibana

安部直樹 Naoki Abe

飯尾次郎 Jiro Iio

境 洋人 Hiroto Sakai

佐野恵津子 Etsuko Sano

nmp 98
(Web site Japanese version)

貝島桃代 Momoyo Kaijima

黒田潤三 Junzo Kuroda

安野 彰 Akira Yasuno

高木 俊 Shun Takagi

塚本由晴 Yoshiharu Tsukamoto

春木裕美子 Yumiko Haruki

荻原富雄 Tomio Ogiwara

トム・ヴィンセント Tom Vincent

橘 淳子 Junko Tachibana

安部直樹 Naoki Abe

飯尾次郎 Jiro Iio

境 洋人 Hiroto Sakai

佐野恵津子 Etsuko Sano

'96 Architecture
of the Year

貝島桃代 Momoyo Kaijima

黒田潤三 Junzo Kuroda

藤岡 務 Tsutomu Fujioka

久野靖広 Yasuhiro Kuno

安森亮雄 Akio Yasumori

大内靖志 Yasushi Ouchi

柳 博通 Hiromichi Yanagi

荒木裕紀子 Yukiko Araki

塩見理絵 Rie Shiomi

レ・スール・パパン Les Sœurs Papin

クリストフ・シャルル Christoph Charles

塚本由晴 Yoshiharu Tsukamoto

観察協力
correspondents

28 田口陽子 Yoko Taguchi

31 塩見理絵 Rie Shiomi

32 中谷 豪 Go Nakatani

33 小川一人 Kazuto Ogawa

34 米津正臣 Masaomi Yonezu

35 五嶋 崇 Takeshi Goshima

36 山口由美子 Yumiko Yamaguchi

37 谷川大輔 Daisuke Tanigawa

38 笠井誉仁 Takanori Kasai

39 小川貴司 Takashi Ogawa

40 小野田 環 Tamaki Onoda

41 浦橋信一郎 Shinichiro Urahashi

43 大成優子 Yuko Oonari

44 川上正倫 Masamichi Kawakami

45 長谷川 豪 Go Hasegwa

46 長岡大樹 Daiju Nagaoka

50 中谷礼人 Rhenin Nakatani

INTRODUCTION

ナイト・イン・トーキョー｜東京の都市空間と建築

違和感の発生と消滅

外国旅行，特にヨーロッパなどから東京に戻ってくると，あまりの違和感に驚くことがある。建物の上を電車や道路が走ったり，高速道路が川の上にうねるように建てられたり，6階建てのビルの屋上まで斜路で車が上がったり，住宅地の中にゴルフ練習場の大きな篭があったりするではないか。ヨーロッパの主要都市では，未だに前世紀の建物を使っていて，建物の新陳代謝からみれば近代化されているとはいえない。それに対して，東京にあるほとんどの建物が，この30〜40年間に近代以降の技術によってつくられたものばかり。そういう技術を背景に，破廉恥な用途の組み合わせや空間構成が都市にも現れることになった。こんなことが許される東京というのは，いったいどういう場所なのか？ 同じ近代の建築術を用いて，ヨーロッパの近代主義とはずいぶん違うところにきてしまったのか？

しかし，不思議なことに，暮らしはじめて一週間もしないうちにそんな違和感も消えてなくなってしまう。

これはおそろしいことではないのか。

身の回りを資源に変える

建築の設計と教育に従事する日常の生活に戻ると，建築の雑誌や大学で使っている教科書は古今東西の名建築を掲載し，建築家や批評家などの専門家たちも海外の事例や日本の古典に範を求めている。それはまったく正しいし必要なことだが，ひとつ気になることがある。それらによって組立てられた価値観から見ると，この都市は，唾棄すべき価値のない建物に覆われているように映るのである。足元に惨めな都市風景しか残らないのなら，素晴らしい名建築に範を求めることも自分の趣味の良さを示すことにしかならないし，美しい写真集も余計な憧れを増幅させるばかり。そうなると，なんだか建築のデザインも急に手応えのないつまらないものに思えてしまう。そんなこと続けてても将来なんかないんじゃないかという暗い気持ちになる。しかし，すでに東京の都市空間はこういった建物によって占められているのだから，そういう現実を避けずに，利点にすることを考えるべきだろう。自分の身の回りを豊かな資源に変えないなら，わざわざ東京にとどまっている意味がない。そう意識して，先に述べた違和感を使える違和感にすることを考え始めた。先に述べた破廉恥なる建物を，とかく渾沌，混乱と形容されることの多いこの都市の現状のレポートとして認めてみるのも良いのではないか。

The Appearance and Disappearance of Shamelessness

I'm often surprised when returning to Tokyo, especially, when returning from Europe. Roads and trainlines run over buildings, expressways wind themselves over rivers, cars can drive up ramps to the rooftop of a 6 storey building, the huge volume of a golf practice net billows over a tiny residential district. Most major cities of Europe are still using buildings from previous centuries, and are not modernised in terms of renewing actual building stock. By comparison, almost all buildings in Tokyo have been built within the last 30 or 40 years, utilising contemporary technologies. These technologies have formed a background to the appearance of shameless spatial compositions and functional combinations, unthinkable in the traditional European city. What is it about this city of Tokyo, which can allow such unthinkable productions? How have we managed to arrive at such a different place to European modernity despite being equipped with the same building technology?

But one week later, these sorts of questions disappear from my mind, together with the feeling that something is wrong.

Changing our Surroundings into Resources

If we return to our everyday architectural life, architectural magazines and university textbooks are filled with famous works-east and west, old and new. Specialists, such as practitioners and critics find their criteria by looking at overseas examples and Japanese classics. This is correct and necessary, but the values woven by this situation judge this city as consumed by disgusting buildings. But, If our footsteps are actually embedded in such a pitiful urban landscape, the idea of using famous architecture as a criteria base seems to be just an attempt to express good taste. Photographic books amplify a desire for an architecture which simply can't be found in our surroundings. In such a situation, then suddenly architectural design holds no interest anymore; the future appears depressing. If we can't try to turn 'disgusting' buildings into resources, then there is no reason to particularly stay in Tokyo. Surely we can start to think about how to take advantage of them, rather than trying to run away. Shamelessness can become useful. So let's start by considering that these shameless buildings are not collapsible into the concept of 'chaos', but are in fact an intricate reporting of the concrete urban situation.

サーベイ開始

1991年、傾斜した敷地のバッティングセンターの篭の下の隙間に、スパゲティ屋の細長い部屋が差し込まれたような建物を見つけた。バッティングセンターも、スパゲティ屋も、東京では別段珍しいものではないが、それらがひとつにパッケージされていることには合理的な説明があるわけではない。ここでのバッティングが通りの向かいのホテルを的にボールを打つことになることや、バッティングで一汗流したあとにスパゲティ屋で食事ができるという利点らしきものに必然があるとも思えない。構築物なのか、建築物なのか、判断に迷ってしまうこの建物に、デタラメじゃないかという不信感と、勝手にやってて面白そうという期待感を同時に抱いた。こういう割り切れない感情を伴うのがまさに東京だ。その感じが消えないように、はじめて訪れた外国の都市でするように、写真に定着することにした。「メイド・イン・トーキョー」という、東京の名もない奇妙な建物を収集するサーベイは、こうして始められた。

ダメ建築

結果的に我々が惹かれたのは、建築的な構成の美学や形式に捕われることなく、周辺環境やプログラム等の条件への愚直な対応を優先させた建物であった。我々は愛情と軽蔑を込めてそれらを「ダメ建築」と呼んでいた。それらのほとんどはいわゆる無名の建築で、美しくない。だから、これまでほとんど建築文化の中で評価されてこなかった。というより、ああいうふうになっちゃダメという、否定すべき対象とされてきた。しかし良く見るとひとつだけ取り柄があって、東京の現実を建物という形式を通して観察することに関しては、いかなる建築家の作品よりも優れていると思われた。芸としての建築とか、学としての建築という言い方があるとするならば、これらはそのどちらにも当てはまらない。強いて言えば事件としての建築だろうか。そういう建物は東京によって説明されるというよりは、東京がどんなところかを説明するものだと思った。だからこれらの建物を集めてつないでいけば、東京の都市空間の特質が浮き上がってくるのではないかと考えた。同じ頃に、ちょうど建築家の作品ばかりを集めた東京の建築ガイドブックがベストセラーになっていたが、そこには我々が肌で感じている東京は載っていなかった。そのガイドブックは自分

Survey Beginnings

In 1991, we discovered a narrow spaghetti shop wrenched into the space under a baseball batting centre hanging from a steep incline. Neither spaghetti shop nor batting centre are unusual in Tokyo, but the packaging of the two together cannot be explained rationally. Despite an apparent convenience in their unity, there is no necessity to hit baseballs towards the opposite hotel, sweat, and then eat at a spaghetti shop. In addition, it is difficult to judge whether this combination is a kind of amusement machine, or a strange architecture. This building simultaneously invited a feeling of suspicion that it was pure nonsense, and expectation in its joyful and willful energy. But we also felt how 'very Tokyo' are those buildings which accompany this ambiguous feeling. Having been struck by how interesting they are, we set out to photograph them, just as though we were visiting a foreign city for the first time. This is the beginning of 'Made in Tokyo', a survey of nameless and strange buildings of this city.

Da-me Architecture

The buildings we were attracted to were ones giving a priority to stubborn honesty in response to their surroundings and programmatic requirements, without insisting on architectural aesthetic and form. We decided to call them 'Da-me Architecture' (no-good architecture), with all our love and disdain. Most of them are anonymous buildings, not beautiful, and not accepted in architectural culture to date. In fact, they are the sort of building which has been regarded as exactly what architecture should not become. But In terms of observing the reality of Tokyo through building form, they seem to us to be better than anything designed by architects. We thought that although these buildings are not explained by the city of Tokyo, they do explain what Tokyo is. So, by collecting and aligning them, the nature of Tokyo's urban space might become apparent. At that time there was a best selling guide book of Tokyo full of architect designed works, but it did not show the bare Tokyo which we felt. It couldn't answer the question of what kind of potentials are in this place we are standing in? What can it mean to think about and design architecture which must stand beside da-me architecture?

たちがいる場所に、どんな潜在力があるのかという問いに
答えてくれていなかった。
「ダメ建築」の隣で、建築について思考し、設計するとは、
いったいどういうことなんだろうか？

フラットに見る

どの都市にもその都市の状況や価値観をダイレクトに反映
した独特の建物がある、というのがこのサーベイの仮説で
ある。東京の場合、とりあえず「ダメ建築」にこの都市と建
築を考えるヒントが含まれているのではないか、と我々は
考えた。でも、「ダメ建築」の定義がはじめからはっきりして
いたわけではない。具体的な蒐集作業にあたりながら議
論を繰り返した。その時に注意したのは、対象を欠く観念
的なモデルによって都市を捉えてしまわないようにするこ
とだった。80年代にはカオス肯定論や東京論を背景に、
都市の混乱ぎみの風景をメタファーにした空間表現が建築
家の作品にもみられたが、そのような表現によって都市を
要約しうるとする楽観とは縁を切りたかった。また、表層
的な様式の混在や、前近代と超近代の対比といった、紋切
り型のイメージに当てはまるものもはじめから問題にしな
かった。路上観察学会が提示した断片からの都市の楽し
み方には賛同しつつも、そこに通底するささやかさや懐か
しさには居心地の悪さを感じていたので、感傷に訴えるも
のも扱わなかった。我々の心を捉えたのは、どのようにみ
たらよいのかよくわからない類いの建物であった。そこで、
要素と要素の関係性をひとまず問題にすることにして、あ
らかじめ与えられている評価やカテゴリーをはずして対象
をみようとした。貴族的／大衆的、美／醜、善／悪、ある
いは建築／土木といった区別を放棄して、すべてをフラッ
トにみようとした。そういう見方が、多種多様な構造体の
巨大な集塊（アグロメラシオン）である東京の都市空間の
方から求められているように思われた。
この集塊を、渾沌、混乱と形容して絶望してみせることも、
気の効いたもっともらしい物語に回収しようとすることも、
ともに我々が肌で感じている東京をかき消してしまうだろ
う。また、東京の場合、都市空間の構造から演繹的に個々
の建物の構成が決定されるということは、例外が多くあま
り説得力をもたないから、都市の建築を捉える時の常套手
段でもあるタイポロジーを試みたとしても、「ダメ建築」が
もつ興味深い要素の雑種性をそぐだけに終わりかねない。
では、どのように捉え理解したら良いのだろう。

Flatness

The starting hypothesis for the survey is that in any city, the situation and value system of that city should be directly reflected through unique buildings. In the case of Tokyo, we suspect that da-me architecture contains hints to think about the city and architecture. However, the definition of da-me architecture was not necessarily clear from the beginning. We debated at length over each example as we collected them. During these debates, we took care to not think about the city as a conceptual model. In the 1980s there was a background of chaos affirming theory and Tokyology, and the spatial expression of architectural works displayed confusing urban landscape as a metaphor. We strongly wanted to get away from the attitude that the city can be summarised by metaphorical expression. Then again, from the very start, we avoided considering examples which can be read as stereo-typical images such as stylistic ecclesticism and contrast between pre- and super- modern. Although we agreed with the Institute of Street Observation's emphasis on pleasure, we felt uncomfortable with the importance attached to modesty and wistfulness. We decided to try to not work with nostalgia. The examples we stuck with were based more on particularity in the way they related directly to use. By treating the relation between elements as the major issue, we tried to see the object without pre-conditioned meanings and categories. We tried to look at everything flatly, by eliminating the divisions between high and low cultures, beauty and ugliness, good and bad. We thought that such a way of seeing is called for by the urban space of Tokyo, which is a gigantic agglomeration of an endless variety of physical structures.

If we describe this agglomeration simply as confused or chaotic, or understand it with a predetermined story, then probably our own experience of Tokyo's atmosphere will disperse. Anyway, there are too many exceptions to be able to convincingly deduce each building's composition from the urban structure. So if we try to collapse da-me architecture into a typology, we will lose the interesting mongrel nature of the differing elements. Our flatness means something more specific.

Guidebook

The result of the observation also depends on the method of representation. If the method doesn't suit the observation,

ガイドブック

ストーリーを被せるとか，タイポロジーを導く云々も，結局は観察された内容を定着させるやり方の問題である。注意すべきは，観察の結果は定着の方法に依存するので，定着の仕方が悪いと，肝心の観察が失われるということである。だから観察された内容を損なわないような，定着の方法を考えなくてはならない。

我々が選んだのは，ガイドブックの形式である。軸線などがなく，都市の境界もあいまいな東京は，ナビゲーションシステムを組み込んでいない巨大迷路である。だから，あらゆるテーマごとにガイドブックが制作されていて，ユーザーの目的にあうように都市が編集し直されている。たとえ事後的につくられたソフトウエアであれ，都市の使い方を組織するという意味で，ガイドブックは第二の計画またはカスタマイズの道具になりうる。しかもガイドブックには結論がいらないし，はっきりとした始まりも，終りもない。そのことも，常に建設と破壊を繰り返す東京には適しているように思われた。

建築家の都市論

こうしたサーベイを行うにあたっては，先行する建築家による建築論，都市論から多くを学んでいる。バーナード・ルドフスキーの「建築家なしの建築」からはバナキュラーな建物による環境の観察とその定着を，ニコラウス・ペヴスナーの「ビルディングタイプの歴史」からは建築史，建築論を思考する材料となる建物種類の選択に潜む恣意性と批評性を，アルド・ロッシの「都市の建築」からは，都市の記憶はそこに存在する個々の建築がつくるという建築と都市の相互依存関係を，コーリン・ロウ，ロバート・スラツキーの「透明性」からは，異質なカテゴリーの重ね合わせの中にこそ空間が成立することを，ロバート・ヴェンチューリ，デニス・スコット・ブラウン，スティーヴン・アイゼナワーの「ラスベガス」からはダメなものを建築の歴史の連続の中に位置づける力強さを，レム・コールハースの「錯乱のニューヨーク」からは，つぎつぎと更新される都市生活者達の欲望と，その更新が生む事件の連続によって成り立つ現代都市の総体の生々しさを，今和次郎の「考現学入門」からは，目の前にあるものをあるがままにスケッチし，どんな些細なことにもまなざしを注ごうとする都市観察の愛情を，藤森照信他の「路上観察学」からは，実際に街を歩いて発

the result often can't be grasped. Therefore it is important to develop a method of representation which doesn't lose observational quality.

The format we chose was that of a guidebook. Tokyo is a giant maze-like city without physical navigational aids such as axes or urban boundary. Perhaps because of this, there are innumerable guidebooks on every facet of life in this city. Tokyo has already been edited to suit every possible objective. Even if they form a kind of software after the fact, in terms of organising the way the city is used, guidebooks can become a tool for urban planning. However, a guidebook doesn't need a conclusion, clear beginning or order. This seems suitable for Tokyo, where the scene is of never ending construction and destruction.

Urban Theory by Architects

Much was learnt from architectural and urban theories from our predecessors. From Bernard Rudofsky's 'Architecture Without Architects', we looked at the response between architecture and the environment in vernacular buildings. From Nikolaus Pevsner's 'A History of Building Types', we considered how he picked up arbitrariness and criticism in the selection of building types as material for thinking about architecture. From Aldo Rossi's 'Architecture of the City', we thought about the interdependent relationship between architecture and the city. From Colin Rowe and Robert Slutzky's 'Transparency: Literal and Phenomenal', we learnt about how space evolves out of the overlapping of various design criteria. From Robert Venturi, Denise Scott Brown and Robert Izenour's 'Learning From Las Vegas' we realised the power of placing 'bad architecture' within the line of architectural history. From Rem Koolhaas's 'Delirious New York', we delighted in the idea that the whole of the contemporary city is made up of a series of accidents, in accordance with inevitable changes to the overall urban plan. From Wajiro Kon's 'Kogengaku Nyumon' (Introduction to Cultural Studies), we gained a love of observing the city before us, and an understanding where even the most subtle things start to hold meaning, sketch by sketch. From Terunobu Fujimori et al's, 'Institute of Street Observation' we discovered the joy of actually walking in the street and finding fragments - allowing the swelling of imaginations and the speaking of small urban histories. We were encouraged to think that each of these theories had been born out of

見した断片から想像を膨らませ都市の小さな歴史を物語る面白さを学んだ。そしてこれらの論が、ある特定の都市や建築に対する観察から始まりながらも、最後には「建築」「都市」に対する新たな認識を可能にする水準へと至っていることに勇気づけられた。東京産の建物はどんな認識を開いてくれるのだろうか？

「建築」から「建物」へ

はじめに「ダメ建築」といったようにメイド・イン・トーキョーの建物は、正直なところあまり美しくない。そして計画学のお手本になるような優等生的な建物ではない。ビルディングタイプとしては図書館や美術館などのA級文化施設ではなく、駐車場や教習所やバッティングセンターなどの B級施設や、土木構築物を含んだ複合施設が多い。そして有名建築家の仕事ではない。この無い無い尽くしの建物たちがそれでも注目に値するのは、回りくどさとか、もったいぶったところまでもなくしてしまっているところである。今必要とされているものが、その場所にある要素を可能な限り利用しながら、即物的に組み立てられているのである。コンテクストや歴史性といった回路を経由して、文化的解答が導かれるのではなく、経済効率の高い解答が最短距離で導かれる。東京ではそういう直接解答以外のものは

求められていないのかもしれない。それは文化が薫る「建築」ではなく、事物としての「建物」である。もはやプロポーションの微妙な調整などは問題ではない。 機能だけ、あるいは他者を意にも介さない欲求が、脚色なしに提示されたような、欲望の零度、常識の外部ともいうべき建物が成立する。たとえば、生コン工場とミキサー車の運転手の住まいの一体化などは究極の職住接近であるが、住居地域と工業地域を分離する計画学の常識からすると、これは悩ましい用途の複合であろう。だけど東京というのは実に逆説的な場所で、こうした「建物」の方に、むしろ都市空間の質が反映されている。場所性を、物語られた歴史や文化によって意匠化しようとすることが、何か嘘っぽくみえてしまうところ、それが東京である。

文化的な反応は鈍い代わりに、即物的な反応は鋭い。隙間だろうが屋上だろうが壁面だろうが土木の構造体であろうがおかまいなくその場にあるものを使っていく。重要なのは、使い方の発見が、そこにある要素に2重の役割を与えるということである。たとえば、高速道路の下、倉庫の屋上、建物と建物の隙間などの空間的な副産物が、使われ方の発見によって再資源化される。そういう事実を、都市環境の中でのアフォーダンスと呼んでもよいかも知れない。その結果として、たとえば高速道路とデパートのようなカテ

discussing particular cities and architectures. They have concrete origins in a specific place, and yet in the end they lead towards an abstract level, which can open new architectural and urban awareness. What kind of awareness will be opened up by the buildings made in Tokyo?

From <Architecture> towards <Building>

The buildings of Made in Tokyo are not beautiful. They are not perfect examples of architectural planning. They are not A-grade cultural building types, such as libraries and museums. They are B-grade building types, such as car parking, batting centres, or hybrid containers and include both architectural and civil engineering works. They are not 'pieces' designed by famous architects. What is nonetheless respectable about these buildings is that they don't have a speck of fat. What is important right now is constructed in a practical manner by the possible elements of that place. They don't respond to cultural context and history. Their highly economically efficient answers are guided by minimum effort. In Tokyo, such direct answers are expected. They are not imbued with the scent of culture; they are simply physical 'building'.

Moreover, Tokyo is really such a contradictory place, because it is in fact these buildings which most clearly reflect it's quality of urban space, whereas the translation of issues of place through history and design seems like a fabrication – This is Tokyo.

Where cultural interest is low, interest in practical issues is high. Whether civil engineering structures, rooftops, walls or gaps between buildings, utilise whatever is at hand. What is important is the discovery of how to establish a second role to each environmental element. With this doubling up, it becomes possible to re-use spatial by-products. The material is not given, but is discovered through our own proposition of how to use it. It might be termed 'affordance' of the urban environment. Further to this, cross categorical hybrids such as expressway-department stores can arise. In this example, the department store depends on the expressway for its structure. On the other hand, the expressway depends on the department store for its validity in such a busy commercial area. So neither can exist on their own – they are interdependent.

Such existence seems anti-aesthetic, anti-historic, anti-planning, anti-classification. It releases the architecture of

ゴリーを無視した複合が起こる。このデパートは構造体を高速道路に依存しながら、商業地域の真只中に高速道路の無骨な構造体を折り合わせている。この例には一方を失なうと他方が成立しなくなるような、相互依存の関係をみることができるのではないか。

反美学的、反歴史的、反計画学的、反分類学的といえるかもしれないこうしたあり方は、固有の領域に自らを囲い込もうとする「建築」を、なんでもない「建物」へと解放する。メイド・イン・トーキョーの建物はそれを狙っているわけではなく、「いまここ」の問題に必死に対応するうちに、いつのまにかそのように生きてしまっている。そこがまたすがすがしい。

隣接性と「環境ユニット」

カテゴリーを無視した複合が思いがけない事物の隣接性をつくり出したり、無関係な用途がひとつの構造体に同居していたり、隣接する複数の建物や構造物が一体的に使用されたり、ひとつの建物に都市と独特の関係をもつ生態がパッケージされていたり、といった具合に、我々が問題にしているのは都市環境における多様な「まとまり」のつくられ方と、「まとまり」の中に見い出される使われ方、すなわち都市の生態である。

東京の過密のなかで、建物の輪郭を越え、カテゴリーを越えた「まとまり」が生まれている。定まった輪郭をもたず、還元的な単位やスケールをもたない「まとまり」は、建築、土木、都市、風景のいずれでもない。我々はそれを隣接する環境のまとまりという意味で「環境ユニット」と呼ぶことにしている。スクラップ・アンド・ビルドの繰り返しで、街路ファサードのような、信じうる持続的な構造を残してこなかったので、隣接する事物の手前/奥、表/裏といった関係も、この「まとまり」の取り方で容易に反転するような、そんな流動的な状態が東京にはあるのだ。

いわゆる建築家的な社会性の内側では、このように多様なまとまりの取り方がありうるにもかかわらず、カテゴリーを揃え、物理的な構造を整理し、使い方をそれに押し込めた、完結した建物が常識であろう。それはモダニズムのもたらしたひとつの方法であり、今やその精度は抜群に高い。しかし、毎日の生活に目を向けるならば、そうした精度は必要以上に高められているように思う。生活空間というのはひとつの建物だけで成立するのではなく、複数の建物及びそこに隣接するさまざまな環境の結びつきによって成立しているのだから。東京の過密がもたらすそういった都市の現象に価値を認めて、それを未来に向けて投げかけることができないものか。そうすれば、公共建築も周辺環境の連続

over-definition towards generic 'building'. The buildings of Made in Tokyo are not necessarily after such ends, but they simply arrive at this position through their desperate response to the here and now. This is what is so refreshing about them.

Adjacency and 'Environmental Unit'

Our interest is in the diverse methods of making and using coherent environments within the city, together with the urban ecologies seen there. This includes the unexpected adjacency of function created by cross categorical hybrids, the co-existence of unrelated functions in a single structure, the joint utilisation of several differing and adjacent buildings and structures, or the packaging of an unusual urban ecology in a single building.

In Tokyo's urban density, there are examples of a coherency which cross over categorical or physical building boundaries. It is something which differs from the architecture of self-standing completeness. Rather, any particular building of this kind can perform several roles within multiple urban sets. They cannot be specifically classified as architecture, or as civil engineering, city or landscape. We decided to name such coherent environments of adjacency 'Environmental Units'.

Furthermore, the external envelope does not act to divide public and private, as in the traditionally understood idea of a facade. We are in a fluid situation, where rigid distinctions such as between shallowness and depth or front and back, are easily overturned by a shift in the setting of the ecological unit.

The magnificent Architecture of Architects retains distinctions between categories, rationalises physical structure, pushes preconceived use onto that structure, and tries to be self-contained. This is even though there are so many diverse ways to define environmental unities. It is a method that Modernism has passed down to us, and the precision of its ways is becoming stronger and stronger. Yet, everyday life is made up of traversing various buildings. Living space is constituted by connections between various adjacent environmental conditions, rather than by any single building. Can't we draw out the potential of this situation and project that into the future? If we can, it may be possible to counter the typical Japanese Modernist public facilities which are cut off from their surroundings and

を断ち切るような更地に建ったり、ひとつの箱にパッケージされることもなくなり、もっと小さくなりつつ分散して隣接する環境を巻き込みながらネットワークを形成するようになるだろう。

オン／オフ

こうした「環境ユニット」のまとまりをつくり出す秩序には、カテゴリーによる分類の秩序、物理的な構造がもつ技術の秩序、および使い方による秩序、という3つの異なる秩序の重なりがみえてくる。高速道路とデパートの複合を再び例にとると、そこでは上での自動車交通と、下でのショッピングは同じ構造体を共有しているだけで、カテゴリーも違うし使用上の関連も一切ない。つまり、この例を、ひとまとまりの環境としているのは構造の秩序だけである。この建物が「ダメ建築」であるという直感は、評価の仕方がわからないとか、有名な建築作品ではないというだけでなく、カテゴリーが不一致（建築と土木）で、使われ方（高速道路とデパート）も不連続で、かろうじて構造体だけで全体がまとめられているという、そのきわどい統合感によるものだと思われる。ここで試みに、まとまりの秩序になることをオン、ならないことをオフとすると、メイド・イン・トーキョーのダメ建築は、カテゴリー、構造、使い方のどれかひとつでもオフになるものがほとんどであった（図1）。その逆に、この3つの系がすべてオンになっているのが、大手設計事務所やゼネコンの設計する完全でクリーンな建築であった。また、このチャートの中で唯一オフを含みながらメイド・イン・トーキョーが当てはまらない部分（カテゴリーオン、構造オフ、使い方オフ）には、パリの連続したファサードが対応している。つまりクリーンなモダニストのビルとパリの街並みの間にある可能性が、メイド・イン・トーキョーの建物によって試されているのである。しばしば2極対立として捉えられるモダニズムの都市空間とパリの町並みは、ここで提出したオン／オフの可能なスコアの一部を占めるに過ぎない。

さらにオン／オフの問題は、材料や設備などの仕様のグレードの高／低、ビルディングタイプのA級／B級、美的判断における美／醜、歴史的価値の有／無、計画学的なモラルに関する善／悪、なども含み込むだろう。この複数の判断基準におけるオン／オフの組み合わせがつくり出すスコアの状態が、「愛憎入り交じった」といった形容に現れるような、メンタルな起伏や、建物の微妙な社会性の審級をつくり出すと思われる。判断基準のすべてをオンにするにはスコアは一通りしかない。しかしどこかがオフになってもよいならば、スコアのバリエーションは飛躍的に増える。

---

packaged into a single box. We can place attention on the issue of how usage (software) can set up a network, where public facilities can be dispersed into the city whilst interlapping with the adjacent environment. Spaces for living can penetrate into various urban situations and thereby set up new relations amongst them. The possibilities for urban dwelling expand.

On/ Off

We can find an overlapping of 3 orders which set up the 'Environmental Unit'. They are based on category, structure and use. If we take again the example of the hybrid between expressway and department store, the traffic above and the shopping below are simply sharing the same structure, but belong to different categories and have no use relation. In other words, it is only structural order which unites this example. Maybe it is not that the example is impossible to evaluate within the existing cultural value system, or the norm for architecture, Rather, the sense of unity is full of dubiousness which is the essential reason that this example is da-me architecture. We can say that when any of the 3 orders are operating, they are 'on', whereas when they do not take effect they are 'off' (fig.1 : Made in Tokyo Chart) This system starts to incorporate all the value poles which seem to form such an important role in the recognition and indeed the very existence of da-me architecture. We can recognise that the examples of Made in Tokyo almost always comprise some aspect of being 'off'. The only vacant endpoint to the Chart that includes an aspect of 'off', is the position which might be filled by the continuous street facades of Paris. By contrast, the magnificent buildings of Architects are 'on', 'on', 'on'. Often, the Parisian streetscape and the Modern city are held to be in opposition, but the abundant examples of Made in Tokyo show that they are not necessarily bipolar. They simply exist within a score of on and off.

Anyway, surely too much 'on' can't be good for our mental landscape. If we switch all 3 orders 'on', there is only one possibility for achieving satisfying architecture, but if we allow any or all aspects to be 'off', then suddenly the possibilities for variation explode to 8 (2 to the power of 3). This establishes a huge release for those who are designers. When we say that we can sense the pulse of Tokyo in the 'da-me architecture' which includes some aspect of being 'off', it means that even though the urban space of this city

カテゴリー、構造、使い方の3つの系に限っても、オフが許されるならばバリエーションは2の3乗＝8通りになるのである。これは設計をする者にとっては大きな自由である。東京の都市空間は見た目上の混乱と引き換えに、このような自由が許されているのである。様々な社会性に対応する建物が、バラバラに重ねられているのが東京の風景であり、だから我々は社会性の構造に触れる手がかりになると思われるオフを含んだ「ダメ建築」に東京の可能性を感じるのである。そして、実際の設計行為の中にもここで観察された事柄を貫かせることで、この都市のありうべき未来のためのエッセンスをはっきりとした形で建物に定着させることができればよいと思っている。都市観察は定着を通してはじめて姿を明確にするのである。そういう観察と定着の間の相互依存性を建物のつくり方にフィードバックすることが、建築の方からこの都市に貢献していく時の、ひとつの有効なやり方なのではないか（図2）。

都市の内側から

このガイドブックは、東京のすべてを網羅しているわけではないし、10年後には古くみえるかもしれない。しかし、東京という巨大な都市全体を相手にするのは無理なこともわかっている。でも、そんな都市でも建物を中心としたひとまとまりの環境ぐらいは捉えることができる。所有者、使用者がいて、それを取り巻く人々がいるということを、都市の内側からそこにある建物を通してみることはまだ可能である。そこでの観察は、現在の東京に対する我々の身体的、心理的リアリティであり、個々人がこのまちを使用者として、デザイナーとしてカスタマイズするときの助けになる。そこからしか自分たちの建築的冒険は始まらない。そんな風にさえ思えるのである。

図1. メイド・イン・トーキョー・チャート　fig.1: Made in Tokyo Chart

3つの秩序　Three Orders

	カテゴリー Category	構造 Structure	使い方 Use	（計画上の良識） （Morality）	実例 Typical Examples
				ON	（優等生的建築） Magnificent Architecture
			ON	OFF	08.セックスビル sex building
	ON	ON	OFF		29.スーパー・カー・スクール super car school
建築 Architecture			ON		07.パチンコカテドラル pachinko cathedral
環境ユニット Environmental Unit		OFF	OFF		（パリの街並） （Paris streetscape）
			ON		06.ネオンビル neon building
	OFF	ON	OFF		03.ハイウェイデパート highway department store
			ON		10.首都高パトロールビル expressway patrol building
		OFF	OFF		70.射撃墓場 shooting graveyard

appears to be chaotic, in exchange, it contains a quality of freedom for production. the landscape of Tokyo is a random layering of different buildings corresponding with multiple social purporses. We hope in our design work to clearly represent possibilities for the urban future by being consistent with the principle findings of our research. The observations can only gain a certain clarity once they have been studied through design and vice versa. Such interactive feedback between observation and design is one efficient method through which to contribute to the city through the scale of architecture (fig.2 : On / Off table).

From Inside the City

This guidebook which captures the living condition of Tokyo, may seem to be old in 10 years time. But it is impossible to attempt to take on the whole of the megalopolis of Tokyo. Yet from the scale of a building, inside the city, it must be possible to see owners, users and passers-by. It is possible to find environmental units with buildings at the centre, within this never ending city. This can become a bodily grasping of our understanding of urban reality. We think that our architectual adventure can only start from here.

No.	名前 name	カテゴリー Category	構造 Structure	使い方 Use
1	倉庫コート　warehouse court	○	○	●
2	エレクトリックパサージュ　electric passage	●	●	●
3	ハイウェイデパート　highway department store	●	○	●
4	シネブリッジ　cine-bridge	●	●	●
5	ジェットコースタービル　roller coaster building	●	●	●
6	ネオンビル　neon building	●	○	○
7	パチンコカテドラル　pachinko cathedral	○	●	○（発生的関連）*1
8	セックスビル　sex building	○	○	○（単一増殖）*2
9	カラオケホテル　karaoke hotel	○	○	○（単一増殖）
10	首都高パトロールビル　expressway patrol building	●	●	○（発生的関連）
11	大使館ビル　embassies building	○	○	○（単一増殖）
12	パークonパーク　park on park	●	○	●
13	バス団地　bus housing	○	○	●
14	ゴルフタクシービル　golf taxi building	●	○	●
15	生コンアパート　nama-con apartment house	●	○	●
16	カータワー　car tower	●	○	○
17	馬アパート　horse apartment house	○	○	○（発生的関連）
18	物流コンプレックス　distribution complex	●	○	○
19	設備ビル　air-con building	○	○	●
20	広告マンション　billboard apartment house	●	○	●
21	神社ビル　shrine building	○	●	●
22	残土アパート　sand apartment house	●	○	●
23	配送スパイラル　delivery spiral	●	○	○
24	銭湯ツアービル　bath tour building	○	○	○（発生的関連）
25	タクシービル　taxi building	○	○	○
26	トラックタワー　truck tower	○	○	●
27	インターコート　interchange court	●	○	●
28	GSデュプレックス　double layer petrol station	○	○	●
29	スーパー・カー・スクール　super car school	●	○	●
30	下水コート　sewage courts	●	○	●
31	上水コート　supply water courts	●	○	●
32	墓遺路　graveyard tunnel	●	○	○（発生的関連）
33	アメ横空中寺　ameyoko flying temple	●	●	●
34	商店壁　shopping wall/mall	●	○	●
35	レールミュージアム　rail museum	●	○	●

No.	名称	name			
36	ツイン下水衛苑	twin deluxe sewerage gardens	●	○	●
37	増殖スライダービル	proliferating water slides	○	○	○（単一増殖）
38	換気オベリスク	ventilator obelisk	●	○	○
39	駅のホーム	apartment station	●	○	●
40	ムカデ住宅	centipede housing	●	●	●
41	自動車ビレッジ	vehicular village	●	●	○
42	ダイビングタワー	diving tower	●	●	○
43	シャーシーマンション	chassis apartments	○	○	○（単一増殖）
44	TTT（レゴ・オフィス）	TTT (lego office)	○	○	○（単一増殖）
45	トンネル神社	tunnel shrine	●	●	●
46	マンション山寺	apartment mountain temple	○	●	○（発生的関連）
47	吸血公園	vampire park	●	●	○（単一増殖）
48	クレーンだな	crane shelves	○	○	●
49	ユーレイ・ル・ファクトリー	ghost rail factory	●	○	●
50	擁壁マンション	retaining wall apartments	●	○	○
51	ブリッジハウス	bridge home	●	○	●
52	宅地農場	residential farm	●	●	●
53	物流インターチェンジ	dispersal terminal	●	○	○
54	ロイヤルゴルフマンション	royal golf apartments	●	○	●
55	カーオフィス	car parking office	○	○	○
56	グリーンパーキング	green parking	●	●	●
57	オートデパート	auto department store	○	○	○
58	ファミレス3兄弟	family restaurant triplets	○	○	○（発生的関連）
59	青果タウン	vegetable town	●	○	○
60	松茸型レールビル	sprouting building	●	○	●
61	TRC（東京流通センター）	tokyo dispersal centre	●	○	○
62	冷凍団地ビル	coolroom estate	○	●	○
63	ペット建築1号	pet architecture 001	●	○	●
64	ダムマンション	dam housing	●	○	●
65	ジャンクションターミナル	airport junction	●	○	●
66	スポーツブリッジ	sports bridge	●	●	●
67	スポーツマン・ズー	sportsman zoo	○	○	○
68	ヘリ倉庫	heli-warehouse	○	○	●
69	洗車テラス	carwash terrace	○	○	○
70	射撃墓場	shooting graveyard	○	●	●

図2．オン／オフ表　fig.2: On/Off table

凡例　○=ON *1 generative relationship *2 monoproliferating　●=OFF

ガイドブック形式

このコレクションは東京という都市のリサーチ・プロジェクトであるが、同時に東京の都市空間の一端を知るためのガイドブックになっている。特に海外からの旅行者にとって独特の東京案内になればと、日本語と英語のバイリンガルとした。建物の番号は基本的に発見された順で、意味があるわけではない。始まりも終わりもないガイドブック形式によって、この東京をフラットに提示しようと考えた。

調査方法

記憶をたよりにふだんの生活で気になっている建物の大まかなリストを作成。同時にさまざまな交通手段を用いて都市通覧を実行。これを元に何が「メイド・イン・トーキョー」であるかをディスカッション。さらにリストを充実。いくつかの納得できる例をつなぐ共通項をたよりに、選考の基準を徐々に固めていく作業は、さながら都市のキュレーション。結果的に、我々が求めていたのはどこかに「オフ」な

METHOD
メイド・イン・トーキョーの方法

Guidebook Format

This collection is a project researching the city of Tokyo. At the same time, it is a guidebook to understand an aspect of Tokyo urban space. In particular, it can become a unique navigation tool for foreign visitors, and so we have endeavoured to make it bi-lingual. The buildings gathered here are not ordered by any storyline. By using the endless format of the guidebook, we thought to present Tokyo as an expanding field.

Research Method

We made an initial list of buildings which had stood out in our everyday life. We flicked through the city on the back of trunk routes, as well as various other modes of transport such as rail, ferry, bicycle. And we discussed the question of 'what is Made in Tokyo?' The list became thicker. The process of fixing the selection criteria involved connecting convincing examples and discovering their commonalities. It is a kind of urban curation. As a result, we realised that what we were looking for was buildings with a sense of 'offness'. The extent of our study expanded into the greater urban area of Tokyo. Anyway, by constantly moving, we could gain a slight distance from the burying containment of the everyday city.

Observation was not focussed on the building itself, but was with a slight 'zoom back'. We tried to view the full panorama - the building and the surrounding environment together - to see another facility. For the moment, we forgot the categorical divisions between architecture, civil engineering, geography, and sought to see things as simple, physical unities.

Flows of people, infrastructure is the object of our observation. It is possible, amongst that flow, to find small eddies. Usually, built structures must hold a certain technological completion. But to use it, or live in it, is not

感覚をもった物件で、その範囲は東京都内だけでなく、東京近郊にまで及ぶことになった。通覧手段としてもっとも多く用いられたのが自動車で、首都高速道路や環状7号線、環状8号線、国道16号、国道17号などの幹線道路を中心に、準工業地域、近隣商業地域などの、用途の混在度が高い地域が特に念入りに走査された。車以外にも鉄道、フェリー、自転車、徒歩など、東京を横断するあらゆるスピード、高さ、位置からの視点が試された。時には高層ビルの上から鳥瞰的に観察することも。物件の採集のために、全身の感覚を鋭敏にして、わずかな気配をも見のがさずに都市を徘徊する感覚は、林の中でカブトムシやクワガタを探す昆虫採集を思い起こさせる。とにかく素早く移動し続けることから、日常から少しはがれたような、まなざしの距離が生まれる。

観察にあたっては、建物そのものを注視するのではなく、ちょっと引いてみている。建物の全景と、できればその取り巻く環境を一緒に眺めて、その全体がもうひとつ別の施設であると考えてみる。都市内を移動しながら通覧することによって得られる距離感は、そういう引きをとること＝ズームバックに繋がっている。

建物だけを注視することを止めてぼーっと見る。ひとまず建築／土木／構築物／地形などといったカテゴリーを忘れて、ただ単に物理的なまとまりをノンカテゴリカルに見る。どれもみな、都市空間に参加する物理的な構造物である

ことに変わりはない。

人の流れ、インフラの流れとして、都市の環境を見る。その流れの中にも渦のようなまとまりを見つけることができる。人工の構造物はたいてい、技術的には完結した系をもたざるを得ない。しかし、それを使うということ、そこで生きるということは、そのような技術的な完結性とは無関係でありうる。ひとつの活動はいくらでも複数の構造物にまたがって成立しうる。また、その逆に我々の活動は、建物や土木構築物といった物理的な構造に規制されている。常識的には隔てられている複数の活動がひとつの構造物に納められることも珍しくない。思いがけない生態の連鎖や相互依存が、そこに発生する。そのように都市をみる作業を通して、東京の地から図をなすような有意義な環境のまとまりが取り出される。

データ作成

○写真：物件の発見と、最初の観察をその場所で素早く記録するために写真撮影。

○ドローイング：しかし写真だけでは観察したすべてを定着することはできない。そこでさらに各物件を図解するドローイングを作成。各物件をアイソメトリックの線画に起こし、その構成要素、内部構造ならびに関連する周辺環境などを引出し線を入れて解説。解説のフォーマットを整理することによって、各物件から抽出する情報を取捨選択し、

necessarily related to such completeness. Any single activity can stand astride several structures at once. But on the other hand, our activities are regulated by physical structures such as architecture and civil engineering. Several inexplicable activity adjacencies can also be seen in the same building. Through such a particular process of looking, our eyes can be trained to pick out certain figures from the ground of Tokyo. A summary of our approach might be to say that we 'zoom back' looking for 'cross-categories' and 'urban ecologies'.

Material Data

Photos: We took photos to make a quick and immediate record of our initial thoughts and discoveries.
Drawings: But photos cannot contain all of our observations. So we made drawings to figure out the actuality of each example. Each was drawn in single line isometric, and the elements and internal structure and related environment are

explained by notes. We tried to limit blur in observational criteria by organising the format of explanation. Careful drawing helped us to see the object of our study with love.
Maps: In order to show the scale and shape in contrast with the surroundings, we inserted the site plans in maps. Of course, they also function as guidebook maps.
Nicknames: We gave nicknames to each discovered example, to immediately explain where the interest in the building is, and to express our fondness. It is also a signature, training these buildings with no author to become pieces of architecture to the urban curator.
Text: Each example has a number. Basically, the buildings with earlier numbers are the ones discovered earlier. Of course, because it is a guidebook, we also need addresses. We recorded the functions included in each, to explain how they are being used. These records show unforseen building types with unexpected combinations of function. The

観察の水準にぶれが生じないようにした。丁寧に図化する作業過程は、対象を愛情持って観察することを助けた。

○地図：その建物の規模、形状を周辺環境との対比によって示すために、地図に配置を描き込む。もちろんガイドブックのための地図でもある。

○ニックネーム：発見された物件には、愛着が湧いて、その面白さが一気に理解できるようなニックネームをつけた。これはまた、誰がデザインしたかも知れぬ建物たちを、観察の立場から作品に仕立て上げるための署名でもある。

○文字情報：データを整理、資料化するために通し番号をつけた。基本的には番号の若い方が発見が早い。当然、ガイドブックであるから住所が必要。これは街の雰囲気を伝えるためでもある。使われ方を伝えるために、それぞれの物件に含まれる機能を列記した。これが意外な機能の組合せをもった、これまでにないビルディングタイプを示すものになっている。さらにそれらを都市のエピソードとして読む助けとして、現地で観察された詳細についての説明が添えられている。

○メイド・イン・トーキョー・マップ：70物件のダイアグラムをつなぎあわせ、メイド・イン・トーキョーだけで構成されたヴァーチャルな東京浮世絵。

メディア（定着媒体）

愛憎入り交じった感情を伴うこうした観察を何かに定着さ

せることは、観察を力に変えることである。メイド・イン・トーキョーのサーベイは定着媒体を更新しつつ、いくつかの異なるプロダクツを生み出した。散歩中のスナップ写真（1991）にはじまり、東京でのアーキテクチャー・オブ・ザ・イヤー展（1996）において初めてサーベイとしての体裁をとる。このとき30物件のコレクションが、カタログ、Tシャツとして表現された。Tシャツでは胸に写真、肩にダイアグラム、タグにガイドブックをあしらい、折ネームもオリジナルを作成した。Tシャツではこれらの建物が、人々の身体を得て再び都市に送り出され、増殖することを狙った。この展覧会は、チューリッヒ（1997）でもおこなわれ、スイスバージョンのTシャツが作られた。物件を50に増やし、大日本印刷とメディアデザイン研究所の協力を得て、日本語版ホームページ（1998）が作成された。このとき都市のミクロな生態系を描いたアニメーションが作成された。ベニスビエンナーレ"Expo on Line"の招待を受け、英語版ホームページ（1999）を作成。今回、鹿島出版会から『メイド・イン・トーキョー』が独立した書籍となった。

コンテンツを増やし、定着の媒体を代えていくことによって、都市環境への眼差しを鍛えていく。この作業は、東京という都市の観察に適しているだけでなく、それをどういう方向へ育てていくか考え、働きかける上でも有効であろう。ガイドブックという形式をとり続けることで、このリサーチプロジェクトは現在を未来に届ける。

---

detailed comments help to clarify how the example works within a series of urban episodes.

Made in Tokyo Map: A virtual ukiyoe map of Tokyo composed of all 70 Made in Tokyo examples.

Medium

Fixing observation in conjunction with both love and hate emotions is in effect changing observation into a power. The survey work of Made in Tokyo has given rise to several differing products each time it appears in differing media. First, it was snap photos while going for walks (1991), and then it took shape as a survey as part of the exhibition 'Architecture of the Year 1996', where it appeared as 30 examples expressed through a catalogue and t-shirts. The t-shirts had photos on the front, drawings on the shoulder, take away guidebook sheet as a price tag, and we made an original Made in Tokyo brand tag. We aimed to multiply the

effect of the buildings by throwing them back into the city on the bodies of people. The exhibition also travelled to Zurich, and we made a Swiss version of the t-shirts. The examples increased to 50, in making the Japanese version of a home page (1998). At this time, we animated micro-urban-ecologies. When we were invited to take part in 'Expo on Line' of the Venice Biennale, we prepared the English version of the home page (1999). Now Made in Tokyo has become a book.

Increasing the contents and changing the medium builds up a way of looking at the urban environment. Such work in progress seems very suitable for studying the city of Tokyo. The guidebook format allows the possibility of this kind of lack of finality. The survey will continue. Made in Tokyo is still swelling to this very day.

異種格闘技

1976年6月26日、アントニオ猪木VSモハメッド・アリの異種格闘技戦。プロレスとボクシング、どっちが強いかをかけたこの試合、結果は引き分けに終わった。しかも試合は猪木がマットに寝ころんだまま、アリの足にローキックを見舞うだけのつまらないものだった。こうした異種格闘技戦は、他競技との差異化をはかることで領域を確定し、専門化を進めてきた近代スポーツ？であるプロレスが、「格闘」という原点に戻ることによって、自らの競技領域に閉じこもって、自己言及的になることを突破しようとする試みでもあった。

近代の都市づくりにも分業化、専門化がみられる。その最たるものは建築、土木の切り分け、あるいは建築計画、都市計画の切り分けで、これらは役所から大学の中までも分割している。その問題点はいろいろあるが、とにかくひとつの場所をトータルに考えられなくなっていることは大問題である。ひとつの場所にそれぞれの立場からばらばらなアイディアが投入されて、かえって環境を悪化させたり、無駄金を使っている例は少なくない。本当は、建築、土木、都市計画、さらに造園、農業、林業というようなカテゴリーを越えて、自分たちの生活する環境をつくったり維持できるようになると良い。それは都市づくりの異種格闘技戦である。カテゴリーの境界を取り払ってしまえば、ひとまとまりの環境を組織する道具立ては一気に広がる。

メイド・イン・トーキョーの建物には、そのような異種格闘

技的なハイブリッドが凝縮されている。「2.エレクトリックパサージュ」「3.ハイウェイデパート」は、鉄道高架や高速道路の下が商店街やデパートになった長大な施設である。これらは交通構造物と建築のハイブリッドで、ひとまとまりの構造物でありながら、建物としての輪郭は見えず、細長くどこまでも延びて視界から消え去ってしまう。ひとつの物理的な構造物が、鉄道、自動車の観点からは交通構造物といえるし、デパートの観点からは建築といえるという具合に、どちらとも形容しがたい状態にある。下の街路を歩いていると、上に鉄道や自動車が走っていることに気づかないし、ましてや上を走る鉄道や自動車からは下に店舗があることなどまったくわかりようもない。それはこれらの複合にもっともらしい理由が見当らないせいでもある。道路、鉄道の細長いという物理的な特性が、たまたま商店街にもあてはまるというだけで、機能上の共通項もないし、使われ方も無関係である。ただ商業地に隣接するという外側の条件だけが、この細長い場所の使い方を決めているのである。その結果、このような高架下複合といえるものでは、全体がひとつの目的で占められているのではなくて、隣接する都市環境に呼応した機能が適宜納められることが多い。

「29.スーパーカースクール」はスーパーマーケットの屋上がアスファルト舗装され、街灯を設置されて自動車教習所になったものである。経験的に車が走るところは道であるという意識があるから、建物の屋上が道路の一部になっているように見える。イタリア合理主義の建物で、フィアット自動車工場の屋上がテストコースになっていた「リンゴッ

CROSS-CATEGORY

26 June in 1976, there was a highly publicised fighting match between Muhammad Ali and Antonio Inoki took place. I was very keen to discover whether boxing or pro-wrestling would be stronger, but the result was a draw, and the actual fight was not even interesting as Inoki just made low kicks from the mat to Ali's legs. However, this kind of cross-category match breaks through the self-referential structure of Modern fighting sports. Instead of each type becoming more and more clearly defined through comparison with each of the others, it tries to return to the essence of fighting.

Modern city planning is of course not the same as fighting sports, but it also evidences separations and specialisations. The strongest separations are between architecture and civil engineering, or between architectural and urban planning,

and these can be seen throughout bureaucracies and the academy. There are many problems stemming from this situation, but the most immediate is the fact that a single location cannot be thought through in its totality. There are countless instances of the environment in fact being aggravated by being fed with uncoordinated ideas from differing fields, let alone monetary wastage. So it would be good if we could create and maintain our own environment by losing the strict definition of such categories as architecture, civil engineering, urban planning, as well as advertising, agriculture and geography. This is the cross-category match of urban production. If the categories can be cross-bred, the tools for organising a coordinated environment can suddenly increase manifold. This kind of cross-categorical hybridisation is already condensed into the

ト」を彷彿とさせる構成だが、この場合は上と下で機能的な脈絡があるわけではなくて、もともと自動車教習所だった敷地が駅前として賑わってきたので、スーパーを下に滑り込ませることにしたそうだ。芝浦にある「68.ヘリ倉庫」は海岸が近く見晴らしの良い倉庫の構造体を利用して、その屋上にヘリポートのプラットフォームが載せられたもので、別にヘリコプターで運んだ物資をこの下の倉庫に保管するわけではない。これらの交通のための施設と建築のハイブリッドのような無関係積層といえるものでは、それぞれの機能部分は別々に周辺環境と結びついてその場所での存在意義を獲得しているにもかかわらず、同じ構造物に納められる理由は、単に平面の規模がだいたい揃っているという拍子抜けするぐらい単純なことなのである。

これに似たものが構築物と建築のハイブリッドにもみられる。羽田にある「20.広告マンション」は、10階建てのマンションの上に大手スーパーマーケットの巨大看板が載ったものである。この看板は5階分ほどあって全体の3分の1を占め、通常の感覚からすると明らかに肥大化しており、むしろマンションの方を看板の基壇という従属的な存在にみせている。しかしこの看板を目当てにやって来ても、どこにもスーパーマーケットはない。それが問題にならないのは、この看板が羽田空港の滑走路を向いており、旅客機の窓から眺められることを目的としているからである。これら構築物と建築のハイブリッドでは、要素としての大きさがだいたい揃っているので、無関係な要素がドッキングされて、無理矢理ひとつの建物になっているように見える。

無関係積層は神社仏閣にも容赦なくおそいかかる。「32.墓道路」は墓の下がえぐられてトンネルになっているもので、幽霊がよくでるとの噂から幽霊トンネルといわれている。「45.トンネル神社」は東北新幹線が開通したおかげで、トンネルの上になってしまった神社である。これらは後から計画された交通網と古い街の構造との衝突が、矛盾したままに定着された姿とみることができるし、結果だけをみれば交通構造物に対する墓地や神社仏閣の無関係積層といえる。「34.商店崖」は、崖の垂直面が建築化されたようなもので、地形と建築のハイブリッドと考えればいいだろうか。建築と擁壁、あるいは建築と地形のハイブリッドである。

こういう建築とか土木とか地形といったカテゴリーが混じり合ってひとまとまりの環境をつくり上げているものを、どれかひとつのカテゴリーに当てはめてしまうこともできないし、まとまりを抽出した以上、単に風景というわけにもいかない。そこでここではひとまずこういうまとまりを「環境ユニット」と呼ぶことにしている。カテゴリー内部での技術体系に則った秩序感に代わって、「環境ユニット」では、長いとか広いといった物理的な大きさの尺度や、隣接する環境との図形的な対応関係を利用して、有意義なひとまとまりの環境が見い出されているのである。

自動尺度

人やモノの集中による地価の上昇のためだろうか、東京には空白を見ると「もったいない」とつい思ってしまうような、

buildings of Made in Tokyo.
Examples of cross between infrastructure and architecture:
2. electric passage
3. highway department store
29. super car school
68. heli-warehouse
Examples of cross between commercial structure and architecture:
5 . roller coaster building
6 . neon building
20. billboard apartment house
Examples of cross between constructed ground and architecture:
32. graveyard tunnel
45. tunnel shrine

Examples of cross between retaining wall and architecture:
34. shopping wall/mall
50. retaining wall apartments
64. dam housing
Even in the landscape of Tokyo, which is so often claimed to be 'chaotic', a certain environmental coordination made up of categorical crosses between architecture, civil engineering and geography, can be found. There is a clear logic in the way that differing activities are brought together by physical convenience such as scale and adjacency. We can see that part of Tokyo's dynamism is ordered through physical terms rather than the categorisation of contents. We start to recognise the unexpected interdependence of activities by looking at Tokyo in this kind of positive way – as a cross-category match of urban production.

空白恐怖症が蔓延している。だから至る所で、ちょっとしたすき間をなにかで埋める試みがなされている。そこで空白を埋めるのは、機能の関連というより、単に開いている空間と大きさや幅が同じということだけで寄せ集められた事物である。ここではそのように、大きさによって自動的に異なるもの同士の結びつきが決められてしまうことを「自動尺度」と呼ぼう。そこに都市の歴史や社会のモードによる取り決めを大胆に飛び越えた、唐突で即物的な事物の隣接や接続が発生する。空白を使い切ろうとする愚直なまでの想像力、知恵、工夫が、事物の結びつき方を更新している。

「2.エレクトリック・パサージュ」は総武線の秋葉原から神田まで高架鉄道の下に小さな電気店が並んで入っているものである。店舗の奥行きは高架の幅で決められているので、それぞれの店舗は大きさに合わせて、ある店は1スパン分、ある店は4スパン分というかたちで、高架の柱の間にフィルインされている。その結果、小さな電気店が高架下の長い空白を微分することになる。鉄道交通の副産物である高架下にデパートに引けをとらないパサージュが、形成されている。「5.ジェットコースタービル」は白山通りに沿って建つ幅20m長さ150mの建物で、後楽園遊園地のゲートを兼ね、その屋上の長さを使ってジェットコースターが設置されていたものである。ジェットコースターの基壇として土産物店やレストランを含む長い建物がつくられたのか、それとも長い建物が必要になったからついでにジェットコースターを載せることにしたのか定かではないとこ

ろが面白い。このジェットコースターの醍醐味には、白山通りを並走する車とスピードを競い合うことも含まれている。

「13.バス団地」は都営バスの車庫の上に、板状のヴォリュームの都営住宅が建つものである。構造の1ユニットはバス2台が駐車できる幅と奥行きで決まっており、住戸部分になるとここに2戸が納められている。つまり、住宅の奥行き、幅はほぼバスと同じなのである。都営住宅の標準サイズがバスの大きさで決められたとすると、なかなかブラックである。

異種格闘技としても触れた「29.スーパー・カー・スクール」はスーパーの屋上に自動車教習所というように、まったく関係ないものがたまたま同じ面積は使えるということで重ねられる超合理主義の典型である。

「39.駅のホーム」は私鉄流山線の駅のホームといっしょに集合住宅が建てられたものだが、ここでは集合住宅の1階にあるタクシー駐車場脇に、それと同じ長さでプラットフォームがつくられ、さらにその上部に集合住宅の積層した外部廊下が張り出している。駅のプラットフォームと、集合住宅の外部廊下が、吹きさらしの細長い空間という形式的な類似性によって等価に扱われている。駅から徒歩0分。多少はうるさいが、自分の部屋の前の廊下でおしゃべりしながら、電車を待つこともできるようだ。「60.松茸型レールビル」は鉄道の地下化によって地上に生じた細長い敷地に、松の根っこの上に生える松茸のように、生まれた低層で軽量な駅ビル群である。線路の幅をいっぱいに使い、

AUTOMATIC SCALING

Because of inflationary land prices, there is a 'void phobia' in Tokyo, which instils a reaction of 'what a waste!' when we see any unused space. Everywhere, the desire to find and fill gaps can be seen. What occurs in these openings is not usually related to the function of the host facility, but rather answers to a super-rationalism where the filling is matched to the gap simply according to size and proportion. Let's call the idea of the chance meeting of differing objects, purely given by measurements, 'automatic scaling'. At this point is born the kind of building with unexpected practicality of adjacency and connection, boldly ignoring and jumping beyond the history and social mode of the city. The knowledge, invention and imagination summoned in fully utilising these spaces to the extent of stubborn honesty,

makes possible new urban relations.

Examples of auto-width:

2. electric passage

5. roller coaster building

13. bus housing

60. sprouting building

Examples of auto-breadth:

20. billboard apartment house

29. super car school

Examples of auto-length:

39. apartment station

In other words, there is a prescription for 'void phobia'. We just need to find anything of the right size, and try to fill the available space. The insight of the urban observer is tested in their sense and efficiency in working out how to gain

駅前の地の利を生かして、スーパー、ビデオレンタル・ショップ、レンタカーといった、店舗が線状に納められている。これは私鉄の地下化が行われた所ではよく見られるもので、ファーストフード店が入る確立が非常に高い。
東京のなかに空白を見つけても心配することはない。まちのなかで、それと同じ大きさのものを探してきて、遠慮なしに埋めてみればいいのだ。どうしたら空白を無駄なく使い切れるかに、都市生活者としてのセンスが問われている。

ペットサイズ

東京のまちにあるものの大きさはさまざまだが、ほかの都市と比べて特徴的なのが自動販売機ぐらいのサイズである。東京でこれほど多く見られる自動販売機であるが、あまり外国の都市では見られない。それは都市の治安の違いによるものでもあるが、同時に都市にもともと備わっているスケール感から生まれる違いでもあると思われる。たとえば日本では隣地との境界線上に建設することは許されていないが、敷地が狭い場合は当然できるだけ大きく建てようとするので、建物と建物の間に誰が使うでもない（猫が使う）すき間が発生している。ここを使いたくなるのも地価の高い東京では当然のことだろう。おそらく自動販売機はその救世主のひとつであって、現在の東京にみられる極薄だったり、背が低かったりするさまざまなプロポーションの自動販売機は、すき間を埋めることへの対応の結果に違いない。ほかにもカラオケボックスとか、機械式駐車場、看板などが、そういった都市のすき間に入り込むため

の特有のサイズの開発にあたっている。それらは建築と呼ぶには小さく、家具と呼ぶには大きく、建物の内部にも、まちの片隅にも、都市のペットのごとく変幻自在に入り込んで、どこもかしこも同じ状態（スーパー・インテリア？）にしてしまう。メイド・イン・トーキョーにはこの極小＝ペットサイズの効果を発揮して、都市に深く潜入したものがみられる。
「8.セックスビル」は新宿歌舞伎町にみられる雑居ビルのひとつだが、各階ごとに異なる風俗店が入っていて、それぞれの階はさらに小さな個室に分割されている。まさに極小であるこの個室は、その内部の意匠はどうあれベッドがちょうど入るとか、椅子と電話が置けるぐらいの大きさしかない。どんな建物でも極小の個室へと細分化されるならば、結局は個室の目くるめく連結という定常状態に落ち着くことになる。巨大なオフィスビルでも、小さなペンシルビルでもいいから、それを極小の個室に細分化すれば成立してしまうところがこのビルディングタイプの強みでもある。だから風俗店は、建物の殻がどんな大きさや形であろうとおかまいなくどこでも入り込めるのだ。「9.カラオケホテル」もこれと同じ原理でできている。カラオケボックスもテレビモニター、カラオケマシーン、テーブル、ソファーといった必須アイテムを置くことができる大きさがあれば十分である。カラオケボックスの場合、この極小個室の配列は既往のビルディングタイプの形式を参照することが多い。例えば、カラオケボックスが縦に積まれたタワー型、2階の外部廊下式で横に並べられたアパート型、それがさらに高層

maximum utility from these void spaces.

PET SIZE

The city of Tokyo displays a whole range of sizes, but as a specific characteristic, items around the size of a vending machine can be pointed out. In Japan, vending machines are so abundant, but they are not nearly so visible in other countries. This difference may be due to the extent of public security in various cities, but it is also due to the nature of the sense of scale which exists in each location. For example, the urban code of Tokyo stipulates that neighbours must accept any new building work if it retains 500mm distance from the boundary. Of course everyone's site is too small, and so they try to build to the maximum possible extent. Tiny slivers of space between buildings, which can

only be utilised by cats, are the result. With the high price of land in Tokyo, eventually these spaces become desirable for use. Maybe the vending machine is a kind of saviour in this situation. In particular, the very thin or very low proportions which can sometimes be seen are probably because of this tendency towards filling all gaps. Other types such as the karaoke box, car parking machines and signboards have also developed a unique size so as to be able to slip into these spare spaces. These items are a bit too small to be recognised as architecture, but a bit bigger than furniture. They are the kind of size which can exist in the corner of a room, or in the corner of the city, turning the urban environment into a 'superinterior'. The items' constant suppleness to fit their surroundings makes them like the pets of the city. So we can say that smallness = pet size.

化して内部廊下で繋がれたホテル型という具合に、状況に合わせてその集合の形式は変る。「11.大使館ビル」は東京の高い地価のために、十分な財力のない国の大使館が同じ建物をシェアしたものである。ビル全体が治外法権の連合国、壁や床が国境線に相当する。隣国への交渉も、隣の部屋をノックするだけかもしれないし、トイレでの雑談が国際交流（？）になるかもしれない。そんなバリアのない、身軽な大使館はグローバルな時代には格好の形式といえないか。これらは極小が建物内部の細分化に現れた例である。

「44.TTT（レゴオフィス）」はコンテナ倉庫の事務所ビルだが、そこにあるコンテナのいくつかに鉄骨階段、アルミサッシ、アンテナ、太陽熱パネルが唐突に出会って、事務所になっただけのものである。コンテナは何を入れても自由だから、窓や、水道・電気などの設備にプラグインすれば、人間を納める極小サイズの居住空間になる。「52.宅地農場」は練馬の住宅地の真ん中に取り残された畑に建つ野菜売りのキオスクである。それは小さい建物だが、周りに住む住人と野菜畑を結びつける重要なインターフェイスになっている。通常、収穫された野菜は市場に輸送され、それが小売り店に並び、やっと各家庭にたどり着くといった過程がとられているが、ここでは物流の中間行程がいっさい省かれて、野菜は畑から近所の食卓へ直接移される。こんな産地直送システムは、取り残された近郊農家だからこそ成立するものである。極小サイズのキオスクが、住宅地と農地の共存を助け、独特の密度感をこの地域にもたらし

ている。「63.ペット建築1号」は三つ又の道に挟まれた三角形の狭小敷地に立つ建物で、その外壁にはさまざまな種類の自動販売機が張り付けられている。建物の小ささゆえにその存在感は大きく、自動販売機によるファサードの武装になっている。これらは極小がその外形として現れた例である。これほど小さくなると、どこかふつうの建物に対するのとは違う独特の愛着や身体感覚、距離感覚を見る人にひきおこさせるようになる。また、こうした極小建築の成立背景には、道路と鉄道や河川のズレが生むスキマのような敷地があることを考えればペット建築は、都市と生身の身体のインターフェイスとして、非常にメンタルでデリケートな建築の表現を担うひとつの建築ジャンルを形成することができるのではないか。

極小＝ペットサイズ。小ささゆえに都市のなかで自由に振る舞えるサイズ。東京のまちにあふれるこのペット的なものを都市と身体のインターフェイスとして捉え、都市環境を快適になるようにカスタマイズする道具として、利用するべきだと思うのである。

物流都市

海外からの来客に、東京のありのままの姿を見せたいと思ったら、首都高速道路を走るとよい。ナショナルイベントである東京オリンピックにあわせて急造され、公用地や公園、お堀、川などを中心に配置計画された首都高速道路は、都市にプラグインされたローラーコースターのようなものである。そこからは東京の地形とビル群の関係だけでなく、

Examples of spatial dice and mix:

8. sex building

9. karaoke hotel

11. embassies building

44. TTT (lego office)

52. residential farm

63. pet architecture 001

Smallness is a size which allows a freedom in urban action. If we consciously consider the abounding pet sized objects of Tokyo as an interface between the city and the human body, then our urban environment can become more and more comfortable.

LOGISTICAL URBANITY

If we wanted to show a visitor from another country the real

Tokyo, then driving along the expressways would be highly recommended. Because the expressways were constructed in a hurry to be in time for the Tokyo Olympics, they are mainly sited over public land, parks, the palace moat and rivers. They allow views of a raw Tokyo like a roller coaster plugged into the city. It is possible to glimpse parts of the mechanisms which support the huge logistics of transporting people and large numbers of physical objects. What Le Corbusier looked at with the planning for Algiers and Marinetti proposed in his Futurist work, becomes actually constructed here, and linked to make an extensive network. In Japan, the 20 or so years between 1966 and 1988 saw the number of cars increase by 6.25 times, but the length of road only increased by 1.12 times. Transport infrastructure which allows physical distributions is like the blood vessel

人や物資の大量輸送のメカニズムの一端など、生の東京を観覧することができる。かつてル・コルビュジエがアルジェの都市計画で、マリネッティが未来派宣言の中で予見した、高速交通機関によってサポートされたダイナミックな都市空間が、現実に完成し、ネットワークを形成している。それもそのはずで、日本では物流費はGNPの10％にも達する。特に宅急便のシステムはこの20年間で爆発的に拡大し、現在では取り扱う荷物量は16億個を超えている。そのシステムは街角のコンビニエンスストア、八百屋、クリーニング店を取り次ぎに、集配センター、集配ベース、トラック、ワゴン車、高速道路、無線、インターネットなどのさまざまな道具を駆使して組み立てられている。当然車の増えた1966年〜1988年の約20年間で、車の保有台数は6.25倍になっている。しかし道路の実延長は1.12倍にしか増えなかった。都市を生物に喩えれば、交通は諸器官を結ぶ血管のようなもの。そこを流れる血液（車）が激増したにもかかわらず、血管（道路）はほぼそのままなのである。血管が破裂しそうな状態を、ラドバーン原理（歩車分離）という計画学的な手術で乗り切ろうとするには無理がある。そこで必然的に血管は諸器官の中を侵しはじめる。内臓にいきなり縫合された血管とその血管に酸素を送り込む加給機のワンセットが剥き出しの状態のまま脈動するようなものである。建物の中に道路が入り込み、折り畳まれていくのである。車とは隔離した歩行空間の快適に代わって、自動車、電車などの交通空間と混合による刺激が強まる。アクセシビリティ、他の場所への繋がりを快適とす

る新しい原理が選択される。人々によって交通空間とヒューマンスペースの融合は「物流都市」の掟（？）として受け入れられはじめているのではないか。

物流ネットワークの発達は都市に重大な変革をもたらし、現実の都市の形態の決定要素のひとつとなった。メイド・イン・トーキョーの建物のいくつかはそうした変革を反映するものとなっている。

「16.カータワー」、「18.物流コンプレックス」、「23.配送スパイラル」、「25.タクシービル」、「26.トラックタワー」、「59.青果タウン」、「61.TRC」。皆、自動車交通と強い関係をもつ建物である。これらは、物流会社や自動車メーカー、タクシー会社、青果市場などの社屋兼駐車スペースになっている建築で、自動車は人と同じように建築に進入し、スロープを使って道路とは異なるレベルにあるスラブへも到達する。やりようによっては、車から降りなくてもすべての用が足せるかもしれない。車を降りて目的の建物に入るというシークエンスがここではなくなっている。こうしたスロープや、それに接続したスラブは、螺旋や棚のような独特の形状によって、道路を建物の中に立体的に折り込むことで、物理的に足りない道路距離を都市に付加する。内部では、駐車、修理、荷物の仕分けなどの活動が行われ、都市全体の物流回路の中のコンデンサーのような働きをしている。

これに対して都市全体の物流回路の中で自動車が一時経由できるピットイン設備として成立するものもある。「10.首都高パトロールビル」は首都高速道路に自動車走行レベル

system connecting organs for the city. For Tokyo, which is on the brink of sclerosis, it is apparent that Radburn's planning theory of separating cars and pedestrians is completely impractical. By necessity, cars have entered into the realms of people. Previously, the criteria for comfort was seen as separation of the traffic space of cars and trains, and human space. But now a mixture between them occurs, which has become accepted as a new norm. The contemporary principle is about being able to clearly imagine how to connect to any particular location, and have easy access to the goal. Probably, the people of Tokyo have accepted the mixture of traffic space and human space, almost as a version of an 'urban regulation'.

In this way, traffic space has intruded into architecture in

order to allow the execution of the highly developed goods transportation systems. The organ which is abruptly connected to the artery and the pump which pushes oxygen to that artery is exposed and pulsating in the urban environment as a single entity. The architectural design of this revealed figure is also exciting. The development of the logistics network has affected a huge change, and is one of the defining elements which has shaped the form of the city. Several of the buildings of Made in Tokyo reflect this kind of change and beautifully condense the dynamism of this city.

Examples of buildings united with the expressway

13, highway department store.

Examples of the integration of architectural floor plate and roadway:

16. car tower

でパトロールカー発着場とその管理施設が接続し、さらに
その上に職員の宿舎が積層されたもので、首都高速に直
結する特権的な建物といえる。「28. GSデュプレックス」
は立体交差するふたつの道路それぞれに対応したガソリ
ンスタンドが、陸橋のたもとで上下に積層され、さらにその
上にガソリン会社のオフィスを積層させたものである。
「65. ジャンクションターミナル」は空港に向かう幾本かの
高速道路に包まれた空航ターミナル施設で、道路と高速道
路の積層にまぎれているので、街を歩いていてもどこに建
物としての輪郭があるのかがほとんどわからない。

自動車の激増はまた、駐車場の激増を意味する。駐車場
はいうなれば車の倉庫であり、人口密度の高い繁華な地
域ほど必要とされる。当然地価は高くなるが、車を折り畳
むことはできず、相当かさばる。この矛盾を解消すべく、
積層化や複合化が積極的に行われることになる。「55. カ
ーオフィス」は地下、1、2階が飲食店、3階以上がパーキン
グの建物であるが、スロープなどの特別な要素がなく、カ
ーテンウォール風のフレーム（ガラスが入っていない）が外
装に施してあるので、近隣のビル群に見事に溶け込んでい
る。円筒状のエレベーターが7枚のスラブをその中心で垂
直に貫通している。面積が小さくて走行レーンが確保でき
ないので、エレベーターは上昇しながら回転し、放射状に
自動車を放出する。自動車のルーレットである。車はリフ
トから真っ直ぐ出て戻るだけなので、各フロアでエレベー
ターを中心に放射状に配置されることになる。「12. パー
クonパーク」は、駐車場という都市の内臓を剥き出しにし

ないために、人口地盤で持ち上げられた公園の下に隠し
たものである。上部の公園のケヤキを中心とした樹木は、
下に駐車場があるとは思わせないほど大きく成長してお
り、一部設けられたホームレスの小屋を覆う天蓋になって
いる。車のpark（ing）と人のpark、2つのパークの積層で
ある。

これらの交通に深くプラグインされた建物は、デザイン的
に完結しようとしても、決して孤立したモニュメントになる
ことはない。なぜなら東京にばらまかれたそれらすべてが
つなげられて物流都市といえるものを形成しているからで
ある。「すべての道は物流都市に通じる」。今、目の前にな
い場所ともつながっているということは、隣接性の対話の
ような状態を指すと言える。ひとまずそれを遠隔性と呼ん
でみてはどうかと考えている。

スポーティブ

1枚の板を両足の下に敷き、さまざまな環境に放り込まれ
た状態をイメージしてみよう。それが大きな波のある海な
らばサーフィンになるし、勾配のある雪原ならばスノーボード
になる。そして都市のアスファルト舗装されたストリートな
らば、車輪を装着したスケボーになる。1枚の板という共
通事項が、異なる環境を観察し、「環境情報とのインタラ
クション」という行為の事実を知覚させる。ジェームス・ギ
ブソンによると「動物（人）との関係として定義される環境
の性質」がアフォーダンスであるとされているが、現在の都
市スポーツも、身体の動きを通した環境に備わるさまざま

These individual buildings can never become monuments. The reason is that they are all dispersed throughout Tokyo, each forming just one part of the circulation system and only all together making up what we can call a logistical urbanity. 'All roads lead to logistical urbanity.' So, now please delve into the logistical urbanity and experience it for yourself!

SPORTIVE

Lets imagine a situation of being thrown into various environments with a single board under our feet. If that happens to be the big wave of the sea, then we are surfing. If that happens to be the slope of a snowy mountain, then we are snowboarding. And if that happens to be on the asphalt of the street, then we have added wheels and are skateboarding. The common vehicle of a single board helps us to observe differing environments and lets us perceive the reality of action as 'interaction with environmental

な「価値」や「意味」の発見に基づいている。都市環境の中に空白の残余をみつけて、その表面を身体行為によってスポーツフィールドへと転じることで、都市の環境要素の今までにない姿をあらわにするのである。身体と環境の結びつきが相即不離になり、多くの環境要素を巻き込めば巻き込むほど、そのスポーツは野生的なものになる。

メイド・イン・トーキョーの建物には、広い屋上、筐で切り取られ空、箱庭化された地形を、殿堂入り間違い無しの巧みなファインプレーによって、スポーツフィールドへと転じさせたものが見られる。

「1. 倉庫コート」はJRの貨物の倉庫の屋上に設けられたテニスコートである。ナイキのCMで西武の松井選手が他のスポーツの有名プレーヤーとスポーツデパートのようなビルで同じエレベータに乗り、サッカーグランド（別世界）で降りるというのがあったが、ここでも、倉庫とはまったく関係ないエレベータに乗り、緑一面の天上のテニスコートに降り立つことができる。ナイター照明で発光する屋上面は隣接する首都高からは別世界に写る。その別世界でジャスト・ドゥ・イット！

「27. インターコート」と「66. スポーツブリッジ」は、それぞれが道路という土木構築物に生まれた空白にテニスコートを置いたものである。ウィンブルドンのテニスにおいては「クワイエット・プリーズ！」と静粛な中でプレーするのに、ここではプレーする人たちの周りや下で自動車が絶えまなく行き交うのである。

住宅地にひっそりと埋め込まれた「67. スポーツマン・ズー」は、ゴルフ打放しと、インドアとアウトドアのテニスコート、そしてパターゴルフ場を含むクラブハウスが、緑深い斜面を利用しながら複合したものである。スポーツマンというヒト科の動物がネットや柵で囲われた大小さまざまな檻の中で、ボールを打ったり走ったりしている姿はとてもユーモラスである。目黒川沿いの「14. ゴルフタクシービル」はタクシー会社の社屋と駐車場の上部にネットで空間を切り取って箱庭的なフェアウエイを形成したものである。打球を受け止める網籠は変幻自在で、さまざまなスケールや形状に対応するが、ここでは、その網籠の下部がタクシー会社の駐車場として有効利用されている。その網籠がより積極的に取り入れられた「54. ロイヤルゴルフマンション」では、マンション、ファミリーレストラン、駐車場、クラブハウスの各ボリュームで囲まれた残余をゴルフ打放の網籠によるボリュームが埋めている。マンションの廊下はこの網籠に近接しており、廊下から練習中のお父さんを呼ぶこともできる。スポーツ、住、食が一体にパッケージされたこの建物で、お父さんの週末は満たされる。

「42. ダイビングタワー」は、映画『グランブルー』の環境を水槽により切り取ったプチブルーなダイビング練習施設で、工場で使われるタンクの内部が海に見立てられている。水中の窓から見る東京は、海の底の青よりも美しいだろうか？

「30. 下水コート」「36. ツイン下水御苑」はいずれも迷惑施設である下水処理場を都市内に共存させるために、空白として残された覆蓋上部をスポーツフィールドとした施

information'. According to James Gibson, 'affordance' is the nature of the environment as defined by its relation to living beings. Contemporary urban sports are also based on the discovery of various values and meanings furnished in the environment through the movement of the body. By finding residual spaces inside the closely packed urban field, and using human action to turn those surfaces into sports fields, the elements of the city gain a whole new appearance. The body and the environment become inextricable, and the more urban elements are dragged into the sports scene, the more that particular sport goes wild. In their capacity to turn roof tops, caged-in skies and boxed in geography into broad sports fields, the buildings of Made in Tokyo exhibit the kind of fine play which should be enshrined.

Examples of boxed in geography:

Probably, many more different types of sports inspired by the urban environment will continue to emerge in this city. It

設である。機能、管理的には無関係な積層だが、近隣住民にとっては「鞭」にあたる下水処理場と、「飴」にあたるスポーツフィールドや公園のカップリング（アメムチ複合）には行政の老獪ぶりが感じられる。特に新宿の高層ビル群も眺められる落合の「30. 下水コート」は、昭和39年の東京オリンピックの時に世界初の上部公園併設の下水処理場として完成した、アメムチ複合のパイオニアである。ナイター施設もあり、都市の消化器官の上にいることを忘れてしまうくらい見事にパッケージされた下水処理場版のフィールド・オブ・ドリームスである。

葛飾区亀戸にある「31.上水コート」は、浄水場の上に積層した野球場が、隣接する公団の集合住宅によって周囲を囲まれたもので団地の中庭のようにもみえる。各住戸はさながらスタジアムのボックス席である。積層だけでなく、そのまわりの環境までが参加した、有意義なまとまりが形成されている。

これからもきっと、東京の都市環境に触発された新しいスポーツが生まれるだろう。「巨人、バッティングセンタープレーヤーをドラフト1位指名！」、「テニス壁打ち世界選手権決勝」「BMX vs スケートボードのリアルファイト」といった見出しが、スポーツ紙を飾る日もそう遠くはないかもしれない。

副産物

今日、東京は建物、高速道路、鉄道などの人工物で埋め尽くされている。途中、二度焼け野原になったけれど、都市の近代化はたくさんの物理的な構造物をそれぞれの目的のために生んだ。でも、都市の物理的構造物というのは目的＝人間の活動にぴったりと貢献することはできなくて、大抵は目的以上の余計なことまでしでかしてしまう。たとえば高速道路は車を速く走らせることが目的だが、敷地の確保に困難を極めた東京では、ほとんどが高架式になり、そのために長大な高架下の空間が生まれている。また、倉庫は物品を大量に保管することが目的だが、そのために屋上と壁面という広大な表面が生まれている。戸建て住宅の形式は建物と建物の隙間にどうしようもないデッドスペースを量産している。これらの目的を達成する傍ら生じた副産物のような場所は、大して量がないうちは取るに足らないものだが、ある量と密度を超えると、都市空間に対してそれなりの影響力を持ち始める。都市の副産物は、犯罪やゴミだけではないのだ。現在の東京というのは、こうした近代化の副産物が、主生産物とともにごったがえしている状況なのである。これらの意図せざるものの発生を、どのように元々の計画にフィードバックできるだろうか。

この問題を考える筋道は大きくふたつある。ひとつは副産物が発生しない方法を考えること、もうひとつは副産物を積極的に「使う」方法を考えることである。特に既につくられてしまった大量の副産物を、都市をつくっていくための資源として再発見するためには、後者の「使い方」が重要になるだろう。メイド・イン・トーキョーの建物には、副産物利用の好例と呼べるものがいくつもあり、そこから学ぶことは多い。

may not be too far away that we see headlines such as 'Batting Centre Player Hits The Big Legue!', 'Wall-Tennis World Cup Finals!', 'BMX vs Skateboard Real Fight!'

BY-PRODUCT

Today, Tokyo is completely covered by constructions; buildings, expressways, railways; even though the city has twice been burnt to the ground. During the process of modernisation, many physical constructions were built for various reasons. But the city's physical constructions do not entirely serve the equation of aim = people's lives. Mostly, there has been produced a surplus, over and above the raw requirements of the aim. For example, the aim of the expressways is to let cars run as fast as possible, but because the acquisition of land is very difficult in Tokyo, most of the expressways have been raised off the ground, which produces enormous amounts of under- infrastructure space. The aim of warehouses is to store as much as possible, but they also result in huge surfaces of wall and roof planes. The form and layout of the detached house type makes gaps between house and house become a mass production of dead space. This kind of space is like a by-product. Whilst its density stays minimal, its meaning is insubstantial, but once it reaches a certain quantity and density, it starts to make its own impression on the urban space. Urban by-products are not only criminal activity and rubbish heaps. Contemporary Tokyo's situation is a crazy mixture of the main-products and by-products of modernisation. How can we feed back the birth of such unexpected products into the urban planning system?

スポーツフィールド都市でも触れた「1.倉庫コート」「30.下水コート」「31.上水コート」は、やむなく発生する屋上をスポーツに利用するものであるが、同様に屋上利用の例としては「68.ヘリ倉庫」「29.スーパーカースクール」「33.アメ横空中寺」などをあげることができる。屋上を新しい地表面だと考え、さらに、それらをネットワークすることまでできれば、かなり都市空間は面白くなると思われる。

新宿のシンボルともいえるカメラ店。その壁面は縦横無尽にネオンや広告のグラフィックで覆われている。東口駅前の「6.ネオンビル」壁面は、1階が商品、2階から最上階までが取り扱う商品の種類を示す文字、屋上部分が店名のネオンで装飾されていて、空白として残されているのは小さな窓だけである。この形式は店の違いを越えて反復されているので、特に意識していないと隣のビルが違う店であることにさえ気がつかない。このような広告の形式は、何ひとつ無駄にするなという商魂が見事に都市空間に現れたものであると同時に、そのような商魂の現れを良しとした市民のおおらかさの証しでもある。また、文字という記号が建物のような大きさを獲得し、しかも電気仕掛けで明滅したり動いたりすることによる都市空間の変容は、すでに何人かの建築家によって現代的な建築表現として再解釈されているが、そのテクストとイメージの融合したような状態は、今後ますます考察の対象になるものと思われる。

東武線の駅の下が東部鉄道交通博物館になっている「35.レールミュージアム」は、鉄道高架下の細長さを鉄道車両の展示に利用したもので、殿堂入りした鉄道の上を現役の車両が走り抜けていると考えると妙な説得力がある。万世橋にある国立交通博物館が本家となる形式であるが、その本家は煉瓦造りの旧万世橋駅を用途替えしたもので、現在上部の線路は点検車両の操車場になっている。京王線高尾駅そばの高架下を利用した「40.ムカデ住宅」では、約300mの中に43戸の独立住宅が収まっており、この私鉄の社宅として用いられている。住戸は高架の橋脚のスパンを均等に分割するように、同じ規模、形式で規格化されており、振動を伝えないように構造的には縁が切られているので、不法占拠した住居のような生活のバイタリティは感じられない。別々の住戸に住みながら、会社がつくった高架＝一つ屋根の下に集まって住んでいるのである。

この他「2.エレクトリックパサージュ」、「3.ハイウェイデパート」など異種格闘技で述べたものも、交通構造物による副産物の利用例といえるだろう。

　基本的に、副産物はありきたりでどこにでもある物の方が、都市をつくる資源として読み替え甲斐があると断った上で、最後に都市の特異点をなす例をあげよう。高架下ではないが、首都高速道路はジャンクション部分に必ず螺旋状のスロープを発生させる。その中央の空白をテニスコートにしたのが「27.インターコート」である。螺旋状のスロープとホワイトノイズに囲まれてのプレーは、まるでUSオープンのコートの観客席と大歓声の中にいるような臨場感？

この他、運河に掛けられた橋の下が、埋め立てによって地下空間化し、映画館に改造された「4.シネブリッジ」や、私

There are two main threads to thinking about this issue. One is to try to think of a method where by-products do not ensue. Another is to try to think of a method where by-products can be actively utilised. In particular, when we consider that the city already abounds with ignored and undefined surplus spaces, it seems appropriate to try to rediscover these as a positive resource. It becomes important to think of a way to actually use them. The buildings of Made in Tokyo have many good examples of by-product utilisation, and there is much we can learn from them.

Examples of rooftop utilisation:

15. warehouse court

29. super car school

30. sewage courts

33. ameyoko flying temple

Examples of wall plane utilisation:

6. neon building

7. pachinko cathedral

8. sex building

Examples of under-infrastructure space utilisation:

2 . electric passage

3 . high way department store

35. rail museum

40. centipede housing

Other examples:

4 . cine-bridge

27. interchange court

60. sprouting building

These urban by-products; rooftops, wall planes, under-infrastructure, and the abundant gaps between houses; are

鉄の地下化によって生じた地上の線形地に建てられる「60.松茸型レールビル」なども、都市改造の生き証人のような特異点な副産物を利用している。

このように屋上、壁面、高架下や、ここでは例をあげなかった住宅地に大量にある建物の隙間の空間などの都市の副産物は、あらかじめ想定された用途をあてがわれていない、すぐ隣にある空白（ヴォイド）なのである。今は、ひたすら空白恐怖症のようにこれを何かで塗りつぶすことばかりがなされているし、その意義も個別にしか考えられていない。こうした空白は、過密すぎる都市空間で息抜きの場所（オフ）になることも、まったく違う使い方によってリサイクルされることもできる。副産物＝空白とその集合というのは、都市を作る上での道具として今後大いに利用できるのではないだろうか。

都市居住

空気がきれいで緑豊かな騒音のない環境、南向きの大開口からの燦爛と太陽光が注ぐ広い部屋、こんな理想的な居住環境の快適さをメガロポリス東京で求めるなら、郊外に逃げるか、高いコストを支払うかなどの代償が間違いなく必要である。そのような高密度の居住環境をより快適にしようと、建築家、都市計画家たちは、搭状都市や東京湾都市などの田園と都市を共存させるユートピアを構想したが、それらは必ずしも実現されているとは言えない。しかし、現実の都市の居住には、環境条件に適応し、新種の免疫を備えることで都市の病魔を克服しようと試みている例が

見られる。

現在、東京（23区）の就業者の68％が第三次産業に従事しているといわれている。明治からとはいえ、これだけ短期間に高密度に都市化を成就させた労働者、経営者たちにとっての善とは、生産、流通活動の効率性であった。この価値基準に居住を投げ込むならば、「超職住接近」という単純明快だがとても勇気を必要とする方針が導かれるだろう。ウォークマン、カップラーメンといったメイド・イン・ジャパンの圧倒的なファンクショナリズムの究極美がそうだったように、メイド・イン・トーキョーで観察した都市居住の形式も、これからの都市環境における私たちの新しい生き方を教導してくれるものであると思う。

「15.生コンアパート」は生コンプラントと運転手寮の複合である。建設現場に時間通りに生コンを届けるために、運転手はプラントと寝食をともにする。都市の巨大な建設システムに生身の人間が組み込まれている。土工事会社の事務所、社宅が、土や資材の置かれたピロティの上に建つ「22.残土アパート」や、運送会社の車庫、集配所、事務所と社宅が複合した「18.物流コンプレックス」も同様である。大井競馬場に隣接する「17.馬アパート」は1階に厩舎、2階、3階に調教師宿舎という、馬類憐れみの令が発令されているかのような馬人同等の複合で、同じタイプの建物が33棟整然と並ぶ。稼ぐのは圧倒的に馬だから、経済的には馬が主人といえなくもない。これらは、「超職住接近」の顕著な例である。

「50.擁壁マンション」では建物から延びた梁はそのまま擁

void spaces which generally avoid a pre-defined use being allocated to them. At the moment, the usual attitude is a kind of void-phobia which tries to paint over all trace of such spaces and they are considered only individually so that the meaning of their multiplicity is lost. However, these voids can become a breathing space within the over-dense urban environment of Tokyo, and can be recycled into a completely new use – the equation of by-product = void and its assemblies can become a tool for a future worm's eye view urban planning.

URBAN DWELLING

Within the extreme density of Tokyo, real estate ideals - clean air, lots of greenery, no noise pollution, big rooms, plentiful sunlight from large south facing windows, - are like

a far away dream. Trying to approach such ideals entails huge cost; enormous monetary expense, or being pushed out to extremely distant suburbs. The uncontrollable spread of this situation is like a virus. Modern architects and city planners tried to counterattack the effects of this highly dense living environment by taking utopian ideas combining the rural and urban, and trying to project them into towers or onto Tokyo Bay. However, amongst contemporary urban dwellings, there exists an immunised type, which has adapted to the actuality of the current condition in its own attempt to overcome the urban disease.

In Tokyo's 23 wards, 68% of employees are working in the service sector. The workers and managers propelled the speed and intensity of urbanisation, and regard the efficiency of production and logistics as a resulting virtue. If dwelling is

壁の構造になっていて、それが廊下のスペースに露出している。梁の途中から白く塗られて、一応マンションはそこから先と区別されているが、力学的には切れ目がないひとつの構造物である。浄妙寺川に隣接する「64.ダムマンション」の足元は、普段は広場になっているが、大雨などで川が増水すると池に変わる。これは川の氾濫を押さえるために設けられた貯水池で、ここに蓄えられた水は雨足が弱まってから時間差で放水される。常時と非常時で様態が変わるわけである。このように建築と治水構造物のハイブリッドでは、基本的には非常時を前提としてつくられた場所が、常時には別の使われ方によって読み替えられる面白さがある。青山墓地へ渡る陸橋の下の「51.ブリッジハウス」はコルビュジエ風のカラーリングの高架橋の下にある養護施設である。青山というファッショナブルで華やかな地域にあるが、土木構築物に住み込むということには、さすがにひっそりとしたものがある。これらは土木構築物を身近に引き寄せながら住む例である。

自動尺度でもとりあげた「13.バス団地」副産物でもとりあげた「40.ムカデ住宅」などは、住むことと必ずしも関係ないところで、居住単位の寸法が決められるものである。デザインというのは、できるだけ人間のためにモノの方の融通をきかすものだが、これらの場合にはむしろ人間の方が融通をきかせているようにもみえる。但し、ここまでくるともはやユーモラスと言うべきかもしれない。

テレビアニメ「機動戦士ガンダム」では「ニュータイプ」といわれるキャラクターたちが登場した。それは宇宙時代における新しい環境で起こる人類の進化を捉えた物語だ。今はまだそうした宇宙時代ではないが、ここで報告した建物に居住する現代人たちにも、現実の都市のさまざまな環境を克服し住み込んでいく「ニュータイプ」の姿を見ることができるのではないか。

建物としての機械

都市は我々の生活の場所である。しかし少しひいてその全体を眺めれば、それは生産と消費を繰り返すひとつの機械や生き物のような有機的な組織と捉えられる。あくまで比喩であるが、そう捉えれば当然、都市にも動力器官、伝達器官、排泄器官、貯蔵器官などが必要になる。東京のようなメガロポリスでは、そういった器官にかかる負荷は非常に大きく、それを処理するための器官も大規模になってくる。こういう器官を施設として読み替えると、特に東京湾岸などに、この喩えに当てはまる施設を集中的にみることができる。発電所、ゴミ焼却場、下水処理場などのインフラストラクチュアに近い施設がその代表であるが、それらはモダニズム建築の歴史の中で、工場建築として処理されてきた経緯があるので、あまり異様な様相を呈することはない（特に最近のゴミ焼却場は小綺麗にパッケージされている）。しかし新興のインフラ関連施設の中には、本当に機械や道具がビルのように大きくなってしまった異形のものがみられる。コルビュジエによれば「機械としての住居」がありうるわけだが、メイド・イン・トーキョーによれば、その逆もまた真なりで「建物としての機械」、つまり建築を

also thrown into the same framework of this criteria, then a very simple yet courageous thesis of 'hyper-closeness of home and x' takes effect. Like the absolute beauty seen in overwhelming functionalism of products made in Japan, such as the walkman and cup noodles, the format of urban dwellings observed in the buildings of Made in Tokyo can guide us towards new ways of living in the future urban environment.

Examples of living with work:

15. nama-con apartment house

17. horse apartment house

18. distribution complex

22. sand apartment house

Examples of living with civil engineering:

50. retaining wall apartments

51. bridge home

64. dam housing

Examples of living with given measurements:

13. bus housing

40. centipede housing

Twenty years ago, there was a TV animation series which attracted popularity with the concept 'new type'. The 'new type' meant an evolved human who had adapted to the new environment of the space age. Tokyo is not in the space age at the moment, but through looking at these contemporary dwellers, living in these buildings and overcoming various contemporary urban difficulties, I feel I can see the figure of the 'new type'.

比喩にした機械があり得るのである。

「19.設備ビル」は羽田空港周辺の地域冷暖房システムのための施設で、冷水、高温水発生器、クーリングタワー、タンク、パイプラインなどが積層、付加されてひとつの地上のヴォリュームにまとめられている。空港の関連施設全体のエアコンのようなものであるが、地域をまとめるぐらいの規模になると、7階建てぐらいのビルになってしまい、同じ通り沿いの建物と、その大きさやハイテクな外観において遜色がない。正面に横付けされた剥き出しのパイプラインがなければ、町並みにもなじんでしまう。「62.冷凍団地ビル」は、工場でつくられるのではなく、現場でつくられた東京の冷蔵庫である。あなたの冷蔵庫の中身が、スーパーマーケットの冷蔵庫から取り出されたものである以上、そのスーパーマーケットの冷蔵庫の中身もより大きな冷蔵庫に納められていたはず。あなたの冷蔵庫にとっては祖父母にあたるこれらの冷蔵庫も、面的に配列されて外部空間を生み、荷下ろし用のプラットフォームや事務所など、トラックや人間とのインターフェイスを備えると、都市的、建築的な相貌を呈するようになる。屋内スキー場というのは原理的にはこれが斜めになったものである。このように、日常生活の瑣末な細部も、都市全体に渡ってかき集められると、ヒューマンスケールを越えた規模をもつにいたる。このように「建物としての機械」は都市にとっての家電製品である。

「48.クレーンだな」はバブル期の東京のスカイラインをにぎわせていたタワークレーンの寝床である。あのタワークレーンたちはどこへ行っていたのかと思っていたら、こんなかたちで積み上げられて、仮設建築物の様相を呈していた。クレーンを構成するトラスは構造的に独立しているので、層を重ねた建築のようにみえる。この仮設建築（？）が解体されるときが、景気の回復を意味すれば良いのだが。「43.シャーシーマンション」はトレーラーのシャーシーの寝床である。海上貨物輸送のコンテナは6mと12mの2種類に規格化されており、さらに車体の有効利用を考えるとシャーシーの数と種類は車本体の2倍、3倍になる。コンテナタンカーの増加に伴って増加する同一規格のシャーシーを合理的に格納するシステムとして考案されたものである。このように「建物としての機械」は都市にばらまかれた道具たちのガレージである。

1階はゲームセンター、駐車場、レストランで、その屋上がプールになっている「37.増殖スライダービル」は、プールのアトラクションとして設置されたウォータースライダーのチューブが、より強い刺激を求めて年々増築されて、ついには8階建て程の高さになったものである。住宅地の上空に異様な姿でそびえ、子供たちの歓声と若い女性の嬌声を放散させるこのウォータースライダーには、船舶内部の高度な配管技術が応用されており、物理的には設備や化学プラントなどと変わりがない。産業系の技術が生身の人間のための大アトラクションに転用されている。「69.洗車テラス」は1階では機械による洗車、その屋上では人間による手洗いの洗車というように、洗車のふたつの筋道（機械式、手作業）が積層されているものである。洗車という目

MACHINE AS BUILDING

The city is our place for living. But if we zoom back, it can be seen as an organic structure like a machine or a creature breathing production and consumption. Although it is an analogy, if we think this way, then the city starts to need organs for power, transportation, storage, discharge. In the case of a megalopolis like Tokyo, the load on such organs is enormous, and the organs required to look after them must also become huge. In reading these organs as built facilities, they can be readily seen in the area around Tokyo bay. The most typical examples of these are almost-infrastructures such as power plants, garbage incinerators and sewerage plants. Generally, they have been regarded as types of industrial building; because of Modern architectural history's interest in them, they do not seem particularly strange to us now. However, in the latest infrastructure related facilities of Tokyo, bizarre buildings which are really like large machines or instruments have appeared. These are what we have focused on for Made in Tokyo. According to Le Corbusier, 'the house is a machine for living in', but according to Made in Tokyo, the reverse 'machine as building' is also true. In other words, architecture as an analogy for machinery is possible.

Examples of electric appliances for the city:

19. air-con building

62. coolroom estate

Examples of urban tool garages:

43. chassis apartment

44. TTT (lego office)

48. crane shelves

的を達成するために、人間の身体も部品のひとつとして扱われている。このように「建物としての機械」は上下水道等のインフラストラクチュアに生身の身体を直接プラグインする。

西武新宿線の踏切による環状8号線の渋滞を解消するために作られた井荻トンネル（全長1253m、4車線）は、排気ガスを排出するために2本の換気塔（直径7m、高さ35m）を持つ。この換気塔にトンネル監視室や消火ポンプ室、倉庫などが複合したのが「38.換気オベリスク」である。排ガスの煙突であるため、周囲のビルよりも高く、線路を挟んで両側に対をなしてそびえている。道路の中央に窓のない黒い円筒状の構造物が立ちはだかる様は、遠くのドライバーからも視認される強いアイストップであり、パリ市内の広場に立つオベリスクを彷彿とさせる。そのためこの区間は祝福されたようにみえるのだが、別に杉並区が戦争に勝ったわけでもない。記憶すべきは交通渋滞、排気ガスという都市の必要悪ということか？。都内何カ所かで散見される他のトンネルの換気塔も、周囲の建物よりはるかに大きく、生活感のないモノリシックな形態で、しかもその正体をあまり知られていないことが多い。どこかミステリアスで、周囲の環境から切り離されており、モニュメントの条件を十分に満たしている。「建物としての機械」は偶然のモニュメントである。

東京にかぎらず大都市では、インフラストラクチュア関連の施設は、人々に仕えているにもかかわらず、しばしば迷惑施設と見なされている。それらの施設は機械のように目

的が明確であり、都市の拡大が施設の肥大化に直結する。それに対し、一般の建築は異なる価値観を調整しなければならず、単一の目的だけでは成立しにくくなってきている。しかし、一般の建築による凡庸な都市の織りと、避け難い日常生活からの需要の反映である大型で異形のインフラストラクチュア関連施設は、実際には依存しあっている。そのため「建物としての機械」は、スケープゴートとしてのシンボリックな意味を付与されるのだ。このような社会的性格を消極的なものから積極的なものに変更できれば、「建物としての機械」は都市空間をつくる上で独特の機会を与えられるものになる。

都市の生態系

東京は、住宅、オフィス、工場といった建物と、道路、鉄道などの交通施設、港湾、公園などの土木構築物が凝縮した集合体（アグロメラシオン）である。その景観は、視覚的には統制がとれていないので、俗にカオスとか、ホワイトノイズの状態にあるといわれる。しかしそのような解釈は、視覚的に見える構成的、記号的な秩序を前提にしたものであるから、前提を変えてしまえばまったく異なる解釈が可能になるはずだ。現に、カオスであるといわれながら、東京はそれなりに面白く機能している。まるで熱帯雨林のジャングルが、見通しが利かないし、かたちの統制もとれていないにもかかわらず、多くの種類の生物たちがそれぞれ異なる環境世界を構築しながら共存する場所になっているように。だから、機械論や記号論を解釈のメタファーと

Examples of direct human plug into waterworks:

37. proliferating water slides

69. carwash terrace

Examples of infrastructural monuments:

38. ventilator obelisk

In a metropolis such as Tokyo, infrastructure related facilities are often seen as troublesome, despite the fact that they serve the populace. They have clear aims, as machines do, and gain obesity in direct relation to the extent of urban expansion. In contrast, normal architecture must adjust itself to multiple influencing forces, and cannot afford to stand with a single purpose like these facilities. But the banal fabric of normal urbanity is actually co-dependent with the figures of the huge and bizarre infrastructural facilities, which are merely a reflection of inevitable daily needs. The

structure of the machine-as-building has had a scapegoat symbolic value attached to it, which can be replaced with more positive values, providing a unique opportunity for urban proposals.

URBAN ECOLOGY

Tokyo is an agglomeration of buildings, traffic infrastructure, civil engineering. Its landscape is said to lack visual control and is popularly thought of as chaotic or as 'white noise'. However, this kind of interpretation is based on mechanistic theory and semiotic systems. So, if we change this premise, a totally different interpretation of the city should be possible. Actually, despite these claims of chaos, Tokyo is interesting in its own way of functioning. It resembles the unstructured forms of the rainforest, within which there is in

して導入するのをひとまずやめて、生物個体をその生育環境まるごと捉えようとする環境生態論を解釈のメタファーとして導入すれば、東京の風景の中にも有意義な環境のまとまりを、幾重にも見い出すことができるはずだ。毎日の生活の中で実際に歩き回ることによって、都市を上から眺めるのでは得られない、人、モノの流れ、環境要素、時間が複雑にからみあった都市生活者の劇場、あるいは都市のミクロな生態系がみえてくる。そうすればそれらが集積した、マクロな生態系として都市の総体をイメージすることもできるようになる。そういう連続した活動の舞台というのは、建築単体に納まっていることは稀で、身の回りにあるあらゆる環境要素を利用してつくり上げられており、建物の完結性や、建築／土木といったカテゴリー分けは、あまり意味をなさなくなる。

メイド・イン・トーキョーのコレクションの中には、都市生活者のさまざまな立場、趣味、都市のシステムなどがダイレクトに反映されたミクロな生態系と、その劇場であるひとまとまりの環境の好例をみることができる。そのそれぞれはジョークやユーモアやペーソスを含んだ都市の小さなエピソードといえる。

「7. パチンコカテドラル」はひとつの建物にみえるが、実は隣接する3つの建物より成る。中央の尖塔型のパチスロタワーを、両脇からサラ金関係のテナントに半分以上占められたペンシルビルで挟んだ姿は、パリのノートルダム寺院を彷彿とさせる。ここでは、教会立面の聖書の物語に代

わってアクリル板やネオンでできた建物案内看板が立面を覆い、夜になれば煌々と輝き出す。信仰されるのはゼニであり、パチスロで勝てば救われ、負ければ両脇のサラ金で懺悔のごとく借りて再びパチスロに戻るという、都市の恐い生態系がシンメトリーにパッケージされているものである。これは、ミクロな生態系が異なる建物にまたがりながら、形態としても偶然に統合されているものである。
「46. マンション山寺」の境内は、斜面に張り出した人口地盤の上部で、そこに至る参道は手前にあるマンションの内部階段と屋上である。マンションの屋上から橋を渡ると玉砂利敷きの代わりにシート防水が施された境内となり、灯篭の代わりに鳩小屋（通気、排気口の屋上への立ち上がり部分の別名。鳩を飼う小屋ではない）が並ぶ。「41. 自動車ビレッジ」は自動車販売や保険を扱う事務所、塗装や点検を行う整備場、及びパーキングタワーが中央のターンテーブルを囲み、超リトルデトロイトなカーコミュニティをひとつの敷地に発生させている。近くの練馬車検場にからんだ、車を持つことをめぐるあらゆる局面にここだけで対応することができる。これらは、複数の異なる建物が形態からではなく、行為系からひとつにまとめられたものである。

高円寺駅そばの環七に面した「24. 銭湯ツアービル」はコインランドリー→銭湯→サウナ→コンビニ→ビール→「ブッハー」、という単身者の一連の夜間行為と心の開放をひとつの建物内でツアー体験できるものである。「33. アメ横空中寺」の境内はアメ横の商店群を収納した人工地盤の

fact many types of creatures co-existing, whilst each constructing their own world. This is ecology, which understands the creature itself in relation to its living environment. If we stop using the metaphors of mechanisms and semiology and start using the metaphor of ecology, then it should be possible to discover layer upon layer of meaningful environmental unities, even within the landscape of Tokyo. This is a complex intertwining of people, the flow of things, elements of the environment and time; something which can never be obtained by the bird's eye view. Through walking around the reality of everyday life, we can start to see an urban micro-ecosystem, or theatre of urban dwellers. Then, we can also start to form an image of a city accumulating from these variable happenings. This stage of connected action is brought into being by utilising every possible element from the surrounding environment. The completeness of any building and the categorical division between architecture and civil engineering becomes meaningless.

Within the collection of Made in Tokyo, we can see positive examples of micro ecosystems, directly reflecting the values, interests and social systems of various urban dwellers. They can be recognised as small urban episodes including jokes, humour, pathos.

Examples of physically separate buildings united by activity:
7. pachinko cathdral
41. vehicular village
46. apartment mountain temple
Examples of various amusements packaged into a single

上にあるため、この商店群が参道の露店の役目も果たす。威勢の良い売り子のかけ声が飛び交う商業地の上空にふわっと浮かんだ姿はいかにも御利益がありそうだ。これらはひとつの構造体の中に互いに連関する異なるアミューズメント機能がパッケージされたものである。

「25. タクシービル」では、道路から連続する車路が貫入した建物の中に、事務所、仮眠所等のドライバーたちのスペースと、整備工場、車庫という自動車のスペースが、同じスラブの上に同床異夢のごとくパッケージされている。仮眠して、出車して、戻ってまた仮眠して、24時間車路から都市に発進するためのタクシー母艦である。「57. オートデパート」は、直接2階に車で進入して駐車し、上階のカー用品店で買い物をして1階のガレージで整備してもらう間に、最上階でボーリングやテレビゲームに興じることができる、立体ピットインである。これらはひとつの建物の中に主に自動車に関係したさまざまな機能及びその派生物がパッケージされたものである。

　「47. 吸血公園」は秋葉原の電気街とJRの高架の間にあった青果市場跡の広場である。青果市場の取り壊しによって露呈された電気街のビルの裏面をバックボードに、3オン3とスケートボードのためのコートやコースがアスファルトに描かれたこの公園は、多くの若者を集めている。しかしその隅ににさりげなく献血ルームが置かれているので、見方によってはこの全体が若者の血を吸う装置のようにもみえてくる。このように、ほんの小さな小屋の存在が、その場の見え方を変えてしまう例としては、他に極小＝ベットサイズで述べた「52.宅地農場」などもあげられる。「70.射撃墓場」は朝霞の自衛隊の射撃練習場と土手を挿んで隣接する霊園のまとまりである。霊園からはこんもりとした土手（レーダーが取り付けられている）がみえるだけであるが、その向こうから時おり「バーン、バーン」と乾いた銃声が聞こえる。もともと古墳のあった地形を利用して東京オリンピックでも使われた射撃練習場であるが、普段は市民に公開されることの少ない施設である。それはもちろん危険であるからであろうが、この射撃と墓場の隣接が避け難く誘発してしまう、不吉な使用法への連想を封じ込めるためでもあるのだろうか。これらは、都市のオープンスペース、ヴォイドスペースが、隣接環境との相互作用によって、思いがけない生態系を受け止めたり、想像させてしまう例である。このことに学べば現在は画一的な児童公園なども多様化するはずだ。

このように都市のミクロな生態系を観察すると、カテゴリーを横断し、建物の完結性を無視した融通をきかせた環境の使い方というのがいかに楽しいものであって、美学的、建設技術上の統制によって、そこでの活動が制約を受けることがいかに不自由であるかが良くみえてくる。あるいは、そのような不自由が逆に滑稽な都市の細部をつくり上げてしまうことに、都市のドラマツルギーを感じる。いずれにせよここで共通しているのは隣接性への反応が、都市の楽しみを間断なく生産するということである。

building:

24. bath tour building

33. ameyoko flying temple

Examples of the agglomeration of cars and their derivatives:

25. taxi building

57. auto department store

Examples of adjacencies which inspire unexpected ecosystems:

47. vampire park

52. residential farm

70. shooting graveyard

If we observe the micro eco-systems of the city in this kind of way, cross-categorical and innocent utilisation of the built environment can have plenty of fun, rather than being weighed down by the solemnity of a single building. We realise how unfree the limitations set on our activities by the control of aesthetics and construction technology are. On the other hand, it is these very same limitations which create the comical details of urban dramaturgy. In either case, the particular understanding of adjacency endlessly produces urban delight.

VIRTUAL SITE

The difference between convenience stores and other public building types such as libraries, museums and train stations is that there is an incredible number of them spread throughout the city, that they are made up of a small space of repeated design and that they have established a networking system. This network is supported by logistics systems which control informational and product exchange

仮想敷地

コンビニエンスストアが図書館, 美術館, 駅といった他のビルディングタイプと決定的に違うのは, 同じデザインの小さい単位が高密度に都市にばらまかれることで, ネットワークが形成されることにある。このネットワークはPOSという販売時点情報管理システムと, それに基づいた物流システムによって支援されており, ネットワーク自体が拡大された大きな施設を形成しているともいえる。このネットワークというソフトウエア／アーキテクチャーは目に見えない。各店舗は, その部分的な現れでしかない。ネットワーク戦略上, 出店する場所が問題になることはあっても, 具体的な場所の個別の特徴が, 商品棚のレイアウトを代えたり看板の位置やデザインを代えたりするために問題にされることはない。むしろそういった場所性に無関係に繰り返される, インテリアデザインの仕様やレイアウトが, コンビニエンスストア経営の重要なソフトウエアなのである。

このようにコンビニエンスストアの存在は, いわゆる「場所」という概念を必ずしも万能としないビルディングタイプの誕生を意味する。それはどこにでも入り込めるように, 「場所」の問題をデザインに定着しないように考えられているのである。このことは, 「場所」が近代主義以降もっとも建築家たちによって, 建築のデザインを説明してくれる概念として信頼されてきたことから考えると恐るべきことだ。「場所」が問題にならなくなると, 「敷地」の概念も変わらざるを得ない。コンビニエンスストアの各店舗には, 具体的な場所として敷地（ただしデザイン上はほとんど重要視されない）の他に, ネットワーク上の位置というもうひとつの敷地が生じている。これは, その場所である敷地を「リアル」とするならば, 「ヴァーチャル（仮想の）」である。この仮想敷地が建築のデザインとどのような関係を結びうるかは, これから検討すべき大きな問題といえる。メイド・イン・トーキョーの建物には, その検討を進めるための題材を提供しうる, さまざまなネットワークを前提にした建物が見られる。

コンビニエンスストア, 銭湯, サウナなどが複合した「24. 銭湯ツアービル」は, コンビニエンスストアの規模の小ささと場所に囚われない性格ゆえに, どこにでも入り込んでさまざまな複合を生むことが見事に現れた例である。この複合により, 銭湯とサウナは単独の場合に比べて, 情報的, 物流的にサポートされることになる。この銭湯とサウナも, ネットワーク上の場所＝仮想敷地を与えられているのである。目白通りに面した「58. ファミレレス3兄弟」は駐車場を納めた人工地盤の上に, 3種類の異なるファミリーレストランとゴルフショップが間隔を開けて並んだものである。ファミリーレストランはそれぞれがチェーン店なので, 背景に物流のネットワークを備えており, 基本的にはコンビニエンスストアでみたように場所に依存しない。しかもそれが着地する地盤は, 自動車駐車場を内蔵した人工地盤である場合が多い。

宅急便などの小包配送のネットワークの発達も新たなビルディングタイプを生んでいる。関越道の新座インターチェ

between merchants and their clients, which is known as the POS (Point of Sales) System. In one sense, we can say that it is the network itself that makes one huge public facility. But this kind of network as software-architecture is invisible. It is only ever the parts, each individual shop, which can actually be experienced. Therefore, in terms of the network's strategy, there may be an issue of exactly where to locate the outlets, but there is no problem in terms of site specificity in the design of each shop. For example, there is essentially no difference in the layout of merchandise or the arrangement of the signage within any network. In fact it is the sameness of the specifications of the shop design that is the important software for the management of the convenience store.

The existence of such convenience stores brings about the birth of a building type having no regard for the so-called concept of 'place'. They want to be able to melt into in any location, and so the issue of 'place' is avoided. This is horrifying from the viewpoint of architecture after Modernism, which so strongly believes in the concept of 'place' as the major explanation for design. If 'place' starts to lose its aura, then the concept of 'site' must also change. For each convenience store shop, there is not only the physical site, but it is also positioned within a site on a network. If we think of the physical site as 'real', we can take the second type of site as 'virtual'. The way that this kind of virtual site makes a relation with architectural design is an issue needing full consideration. The buildings of Made in Tokyo include different types of networks with which to start this process.

Examples of virtual sites:

ンジそばにある「53.物流インターチェンジ」は、主に上信越方面からの宅急便の荷物を集め、仕分けしてから都内各地域の集配施設へと送り出す施設である。1階は大きなキャノピーが張り出し、プラットフォームが設けられることで荷下ろしの場所になっている。荷物はそこからベルトコンベヤーで建物内部に送られる。また建物には大きなスロープがとりついていて、屋上がトラックの駐車場になっている。この形式は敷地形状によって多少レイアウトを換えつつも、構成要素は固定されている。東京流通センターに近接し、首都高速道路沿いにある「18.物流コンプレックス」は、この形式の中で、スロープが建物の外周に取り付くのではなく貫通し、さらに荷下ろし場の上部に社宅が設けられているものである。この社宅に住むということは、大田区平和島という番地に住むことであると同時に、運送会社の物流ネットワークの一部という仮想の敷地に住み込むということでもある。社宅の部分を除けば「23.配送スパイラル」とよく似ており、ここに運送会社が物流ネットワークの中間で発生させるビルディングタイプのタイポロジーが示されているといえる。

「場所」概念の対によって説明可能な建築というのは基本的に、従来は共同体を受けとめる容器として働いてきた。しかし、仮想敷地の出現は、この働きを解体する。そのことが意味するのは、コミュニティのところで扱われていた諸問題がこれからどうなるのかを考えなくてはならないということである。新たな形態を伴って、共同体が再び現れ

るのだろうか？ それともネットワークによって形成される社会性のようなものが、その部分を吸収し、補完していくのだろうか？今はまだ答えは出せないが、後者の可能性を建築が無視できないのは確かなことではないだろうか。

18. distribution complex
23. delivery spiral
24. bath tour building
53. dispersal terminal
58. family restaurant triplets

The coupling of architecture and the concept of 'place' previously acted as a container for 'community'. But the appearance of the 'virtual' site dissolves this couple, meaning that we have to work out what will happen to the issues inherent in that concept of community. Will those issues reappear as another guise of 'community', or will they be directly propelled into a new idea of 'society'?

GUIDE BOOK
ガイドブック

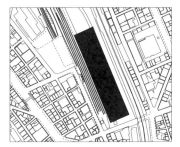

機能＝倉庫＋テニスコート
場所＝千代田区飯田町
○飯田町貨物駅構内　紙流通センター○2階引込線ホームから搬入、3～5階倉庫でストック、1階トラックヤードから出荷○160m×50mの屋上のテニススクールにはエレベーターで直接アクセス○地上30メートルの東京センターコート。ナイター可

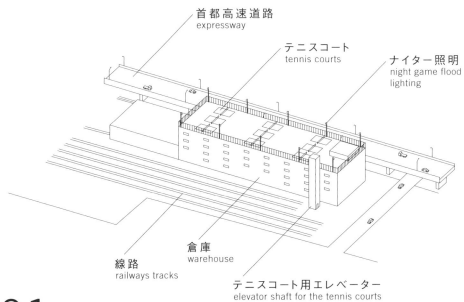

首都高速道路
expressway

テニスコート
tennis courts

ナイター照明
night game flood lighting

線路
railways tracks

倉庫
warehouse

テニスコート用エレベーター
elevator shaft for the tennis courts

01
倉庫コート
warehouse court

function: warehouse + tennis court
site: Iidamachi, Chiyoda-ku
- Iidamachi freight train station, paper dispatch centre
- large volume standing parallel to an expressway
- on the second floor is a platform for the delivery of paper from around the country; the third to fifth floors store the paper and the first floor is the truck yard for dispatch
- almost the entire floor area of the roof space, 160m x 50m is used as tennis courts
- the tennis courts can be accessed directly by an elevator shaft which stands independent to the main volume of the building
- there are lighting facilities for night games which also light up advertising; the tennis school is looking for students

機能＝鉄道軌道＋店舗
場所＝千代田区外神田
総武線秋葉原駅西口前○鉄道高架下のアーチ構造
が商店街のアーケードに読み換えられる○300mの高
架下を3層の電気店の間口が微分○経由しながら神
田まで散歩可

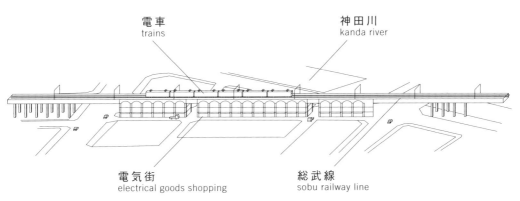

電車
trains

神田川
kanda river

電気街
electrical goods shopping

総武線
sobu railway line

02
エレクトリックパサージュ
electric passage

function: railway bridge + shopping arcade
site: Sotokanda, Chiyoda-ku
- in front of the west exit, Akihabara Station, Sobu Line
- stacking and extension of the railway line and electrical goods district
- the railway tracks become a roof to 3 floors of electrical goods shopping
- 300m length of shopping arcade
- the scale of the frontage of each shop divides
this section of railway into smaller and smaller proportions

機能＝高速道路＋デパート
場所＝千代田区有楽町、中央区銀座
汐留川の埋め立て地○湾曲する首都高速道路高架下約
500mに2層のデパート○高速道路からの銀座の夜景は絶
品○八重洲地下駐車場からのランプと交錯

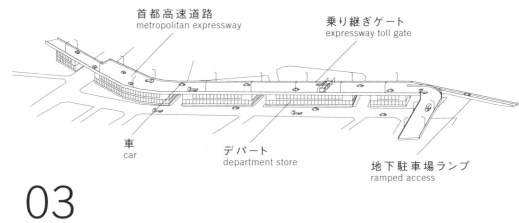

首都高速道路
metropolitan expressway

乗り継ぎゲート
expressway toll gate

車
car

デパート
department store

地下駐車場ランプ
ramped access

03
ハイウェイデパート
high way department store

function: expressway + department store
site: Yurakucho, Chiyoda-ku and Ginza, Chuo-ku
- the department store spreads and extends together with the curving expressway
- the site fills the space of what was once Shiodome River
- the department store is two floors and extends for a length of 500m
- the expressway links to the line of lights from the underground parking facility
- due to the incoming traffic from the parking station,
the expressway is complicated by a toll gate

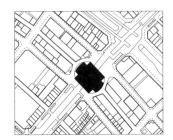

機能＝地下道＋映画館＋居酒屋＋床屋＋店舗
場所＝中央区銀座
晴海通り歌舞伎座の近く○かつての橋の下長さ５０ｍ
に３つの映画館と数軒の居酒屋が並ぶ○通りを挟ん
で向かい合う相似形の店舗が地下への入り口○土浦
亀城設計

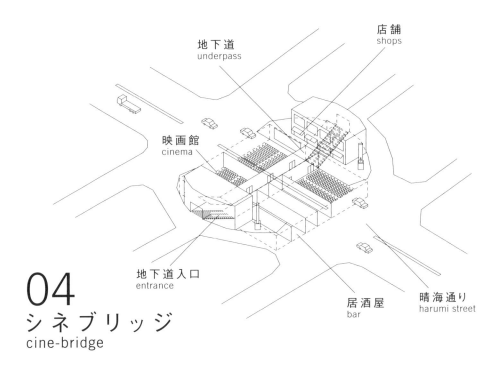

店舗
shops

地下道
underpass

映画館
cinema

地下道入口
entrance

居酒屋
bar

晴海通り
harumi street

04
シネブリッジ
cine-bridge

function: underpass + cinema + bar + barber + store
site: Ginza, Chuo-ku
- on Harumi street, near Kabuki-za theatre
- constructed under Harumi bridge at the time of the river
being infilled, 3 cinemas and several sake bars align for 50m
- twin buildings face each other and sandwich the road to form underground entry points
- designed by Kameki Tsuchiura, pioneer Japanese modernist architect

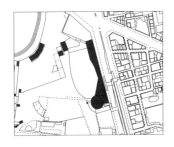

機能＝ジェットコースター＋入場ゲート＋
スポーツクラブ＋レストラン
場所＝文京区後楽
後楽園遊園地のゲート、夜は街を照らす照明装置○長
さ150mの店舗の上にジェットコースター軌道が竜の
ようにのたうちまわる○白山通りの車と並走するジェッ
トコースター○他にもパラシュート、タワーハッカー等、
様々な速度、方向の相対性を経験可

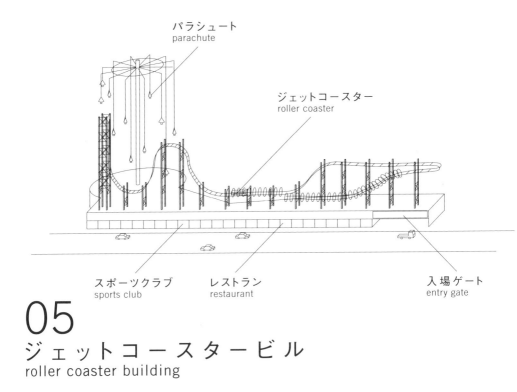

パラシュート
parachute

ジェットコースター
roller coaster

スポーツクラブ
sports club

レストラン
restaurant

入場ゲート
entry gate

05
ジェットコースタービル
roller coaster building

function: roller coaster + entry gate + sports club + restaurant
site: Koraku, Bunkyo-ku
- the building forms a gate to the Korakuen amusement park,
as well as being a lighting facility for the city at night
- above the 150m long strip of shops, the roller coaster railway slithers like a dragon
- the roller coaster railway aligns with Hakusan Street to race with the cars
- relativity can be experienced through the various other movements
also available in the area such as the 'parachute' and 'tower hakkaa'

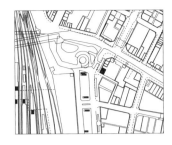

機能＝カメラ屋
場所＝新宿区新宿
○ 新宿東口ロータリー前 ○ 外壁を覆い尽くすネオンサインがさまざまなパターンで店名を表示 ○ 商品名ではなく、機器名を表示 ○ 隣に同じ形式の競合店アリ ○ 夜は駅前広場の街灯となる

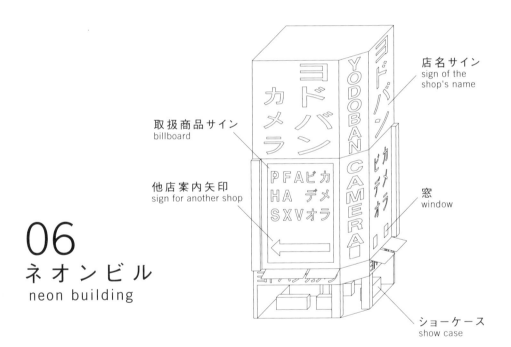

店名サイン
sign of the shop's name

取扱商品サイン
billboard

他店案内矢印
sign for another shop

窓
window

ショーケース
show case

06
ネオンビル
neon building

function: camera store + billboard
site: Shinjuku, Shinjuku-ku
- in front of the Shinjuku East entry/exit interchange plaza
- neon signs wrap the external faces of the building, making various patterns by repeating shop names over and over again
- advertising lists types of product rather than brand names
- neighboring rival shares the same form
- in the evening, it becomes lighting for the open space of the city

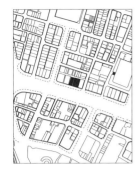

機能＝パチンコ店＋消費者金融業
場所＝新宿区歌舞伎町
○３つの別々の建物だが、あわせるとパリのノートル・ダム
寺院風○教会立面の聖書の物語に変わり、建物案内板的
立面○ペンシルビルの店子は半分以上がサラ金関係○パ
チンコですって借金してまたパチンコして…という都市の一
生態系をシンメトリカルにパッケージ

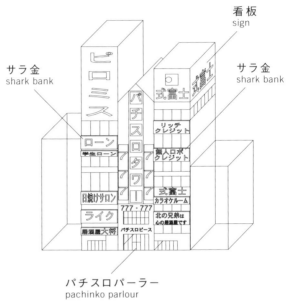

看板
sign

サラ金
shark bank

サラ金
shark bank

パチスロパーラー
pachinko parlour

07
パチンコカテドラル
pachinko cathedral

function: pachinko parlour + shark bank
site: Kabuki-cho, Shinjuku
- they are 3 separate buildings, but if viewed as a unit, they take on the
appearance of Paris' Notre Dame cathedral
- instead of ornament showing the story of the Bible, this complex pulses with
information banners advertising the internal activities
- the tenancies of the side tower buildings are almost completely made up of
shark banks loaning money at extremely high interest rates
- one ecological system of the metropolis is formulated as a symmetrical package;
an endless cycle of losing money at pachinko, loaning money, losing money . . .

機能＝風俗店舗
場所＝新宿区歌舞伎町
歌舞伎町の雑居ビル○ひとつの建物の風俗店による
占拠○ファサード全体が建物案内板○周辺一帯に類
例多数

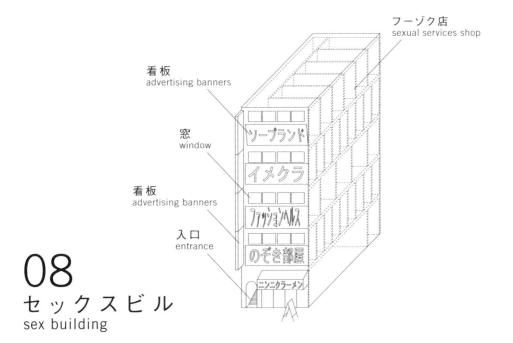

フーゾク店
sexual services shop

看板
advertising banners

窓
window

看板
advertising banners

入口
entrance

ソープランド
イメクラ
ファッションヘルス
のぞき部屋
ニンニクラーメン

08
セックスビル
sex building

function: sexual services
site: Kabukicho, Shinjuku-ku
- mixed tenancy building in the notorious Kabukicho
- each floor contains a series of rooms making up the sexual services shop
- each level of the front facade is plastered by a lit up banner advertising the shop
- this building type is typical in the area

機能＝カラオケボックス
場所＝港区六本木
集合カラオケボックスのバリエーション○他にもタワー
（渋谷区宇田川町）、アパート（杉並区方南）の形式
あり○ロビーのカウンターでのチェックインの後、個室
でカラオケ○赤いカーテンが掛かる窓から六本木の街
が見えて甘美

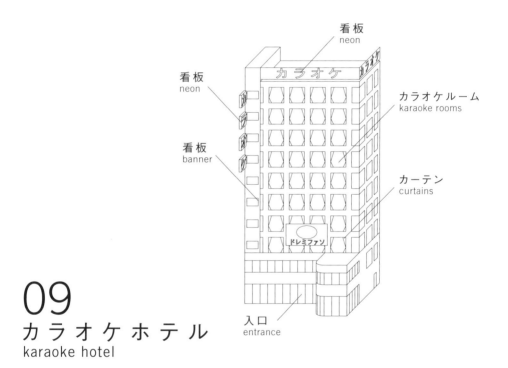

看板
neon

看板
neon

看板
banner

カラオケルーム
karaoke rooms

カーテン
curtains

入口
entrance

09
カラオケホテル
karaoke hotel

function: collective karaoke rooms
site: Roppongi, Minato-ku
- an urban variation of the karaoke type
where the individual rooms are collected like a hotel
- other urban types include the tower type (Udagawacho, Shibuya-ku)
and apartment type (Honan, Suginami-ku)
- after checking in at the lobby counter, karaoke in the private rooms
- view the cityscape of Roppongi through the luscious red curtains

機能＝オフィス＋社宅＋車庫
場所＝港区六本木
首都高速道路に接続する唯一の形態○一般道と首都
高を建築内部のスロープがつなぐ○首都高につながる
ブリッジはパトロール車の駐車場○上部に社宅が積層
する道路公団のビル○護国寺出入口付近に類別

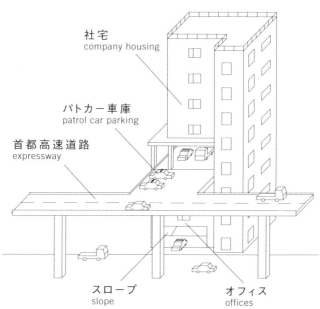

社宅
company housing

パトカー車庫
patrol car parking

首都高速道路
expressway

スロープ
slope

オフィス
offices

10
首都高パトロールビル
expressway patrol building

function: office + company housing + patrol car parking
site: Roppongi, Minato-ku
- the only kind of building whose vehicles could
possibly access directly to the expressway
- a ramp inside the building connects the expressway with the normal road below
- the bridge between building and expressway acts also as parking for the patrol cars
- company housing on the upper levels of the building
belonging to the metropolitan expressway
- another similar example near the Gokokuji expressway interchange

機能＝大使館
場所＝港区西麻布
六本木通り沿い○十数か国の大使館が雑居するマッシブで開口の少ない建物○エントランス脇に並ぶ万国旗が唯一大使館的○東京の家賃の高さを象徴

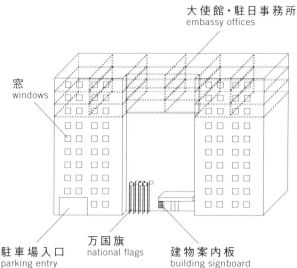

大使館・駐日事務所
embassy offices

窓
windows

駐車場入口
parking entry

万国旗
national flags

建物案内板
building signboard

11
大使館ビル
embassies building

function: embassies
site: Nishiazabu, Minato-ku
- on Roppongi Street
- nineteen countries share three floors of a massive building with small windows
- the only embassadorial display to the street is the national flags at the entry
- symbolises the high price of land in Tokyo

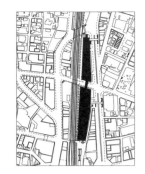

機能＝公園＋駐車場
場所＝渋谷区渋谷、神宮前
明治通りと山手線・埼京線に挟まれて建つ○総延長約
３３０ｍ 幅２０〜３０ｍの細長い人工地盤○上は公園下は
駐車場。中央で道路が横から貫通○なぜか中年カップルの
抱擁多し。不倫のメッカ？

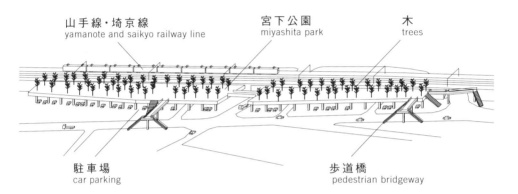

山手線・埼京線
yamanote and saikyo railway line

宮下公園
miyashita park

木
trees

駐車場
car parking

歩道橋
pedestrian bridgeway

12
パークonパーク
park on park

function: public park + car park
site: Shibuya Jingumae, Shibuya-ku
- a narrow artificial ground standing between Meiji street
and the railway tracks of Yamanote line and Saikyo line
- the park width is between 20 and 30 metres, the length is 330 metres
- Miyashita park forms the roof level of the carpark
- the park is accessed from pedestrian bridgeways over Meiji street
- the park continues over the street which divides the carpark below

機能＝バス車庫＋集合住宅
場所＝渋谷区東
渋谷駅そば　東横線と渋谷川の脇 ○ 板状の都営住宅のピ
ロティ＝都営バス車庫 ○ 1構造単位にバス2台と2住戸がビ
ルトイン ○ バス1台の大きさ＝1住戸の大きさ ○ バスと人を
同じ形式に収納

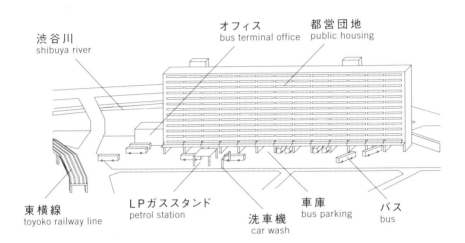

渋谷川
shibuya river

オフィス
bus terminal office

都営団地
public housing

東横線
toyoko railway line

LPガススタンド
petrol station

洗車機
car wash

車庫
bus parking

バス
bus

13
バス団地
bus housing

function: bus terminal + apartment housing
site: Higashi, Shibuya-ku
- near Shibuya Station, visible from the raised tracks of the Toyoko railway line
- on top of a metropolitan bus terminal stands a slab volume of public housing
- each structural bay width allows for 2 buses and 2 apartments
- 1 bus length = 1 apartment length
- both buses and people are put into the same form

機能＝ゴルフ練習場＋オフィス＋車庫
場所＝目黒区目黒
目黒川沿い　区民センター対岸○タクシー会社のオフィスと
駐車場にまたがったゴルフ練習場○オフィス屋上から川に
向けての打ちっ放し○ボールは駐車場の上に張られたネット
上を転がって戻る○夜には発光する緑色の篭となって水面
に映る

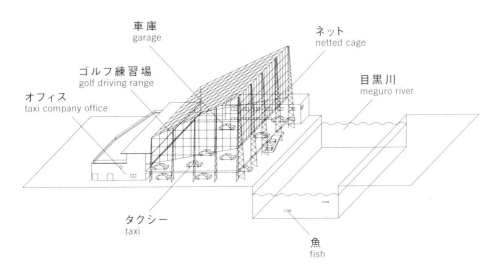

車庫
garage

ネット
netted cage

ゴルフ練習場
golf driving range

目黒川
meguro river

オフィス
taxi company office

タクシー
taxi

魚
fish

14
ゴルフタクシービル
golf taxi building

function: golf driving range + taxi office + taxi parking garage
site: Meguro, Meguro-ku
- along the Meguro river, facing the Meguro Community Center
- from on top of the taxi company office, the golfers practice driving towards the river
- the ceiling of the taxi parking is a huge sloping, netted cage, through
which driven balls fly and roll back towards the office and golfers
- in the evening, it becomes a green cage of light,
reflected in the water surface of the river

機能＝生コン工場＋社宅
場所＝目黒区碑文谷
目黒通りダイエー碑文谷店そば ○ 銀色に輝く生コンプラントと運転手寮がドッキング ○ 下ではミキサー車が待機し生コンを都市に供給し続ける ○ マン・マシン・システムを見事にパッケージした職住接近の迷作

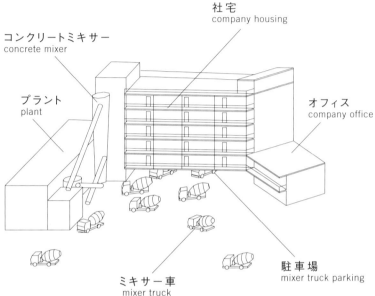

社宅
company housing

コンクリートミキサー
concrete mixer

プラント
plant

オフィス
company office

ミキサー車
mixer truck

駐車場
mixer truck parking

15
生コンアパート
nama-con apartment house

function: concrete batch plant + company housing
site: Himon-ya, Meguro-ku
- near Daiei supermarket and aligning with Meguro street
- the docking together of the silver shine of the concrete plant
and the mixer truck drivers housing
- the mixers wait at the bottom of the plant to service the city
- the packaging together of the workplace
and home makes an veritable man-machine system

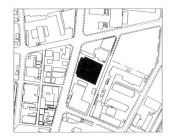

機能＝ショールーム＋オフィス＋整備工場＋車庫
場所＝品川区東大井
湾岸通り沿い鮫洲運転免許試験場そば○足元にショ
ールームと整備工場を従えた巨大車庫の周囲を車路
が螺旋状に登る○延べ床面積に対する人／車比率が
逆転○都市の空中に突如出現した車道

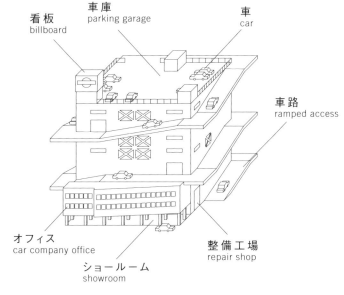

看板
billboard

車庫
parking garage

車
car

車路
ramped access

オフィス
car company office

ショールーム
showroom

整備工場
repair shop

16
カータワー
car tower

function: car showroom + office + repair shop + parking garage
site: Higashi-oi, Shinagawa-ku
- along Wangan street and near the Samezu car licencing board
- single package-building for all aspects of car service
- an external car access road spirals around
the tower made up of showroom, offices and carpark
- a proportional flip between a building's usual numbers
of people compared to numbers of cars
- suddenly, a road flies through the middle of the city's air space

機能＝厩舎＋調教師宿舎
場所＝品川区勝島
大井競馬場に隣接　モノレールから見える◯同形式の厩舎
３３棟が整然と平行配置される◯１階に競走馬厩舎、２階、
３階に調教師宿舎◯馬人同居

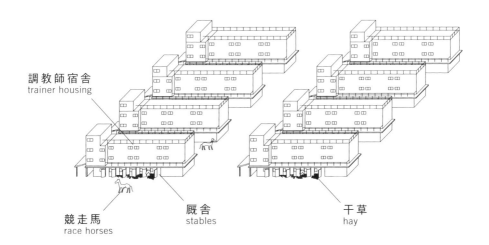

調教師宿舎
trainer housing

競走馬
race horses

厩舎
stables

干草
hay

17
馬アパート
horse apartment house

function: stables + trainer housing
site: Katsushima, Shinagawa-ku
- next to the Oi horse racing track
- visible from the monorail
- one building is multiplied 33 times and neatly arranged in parallel
- race horse stables are on the ground floor, trainer housing is above
- horses and people live together

機能＝オフィス＋車庫＋倉庫＋社宅
場所＝大田区平和島
首都高沿い東京流通センターそば○運送会社の配送所に
社宅が積層○スロープの車路が建物を貫通

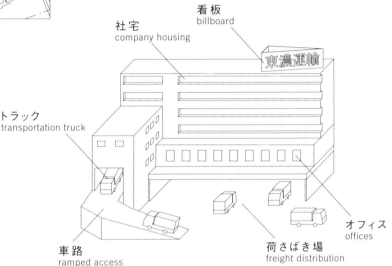

社宅
company housing

看板
billboard

トラック
transportation truck

車路
ramped access

荷さばき場
freight distribution

オフィス
offices

18
物流コンプレックス
distribution complex

function: office + parking + distribution pool + company housing
site: Heiwajima, Ota-ku
- aligning the expressway, part of an area in the city of delivery interchange points
- this distribution company centre includes employee housing above
- the roadway ramp eats its way into the building

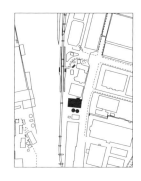

機能＝地域冷暖房プラント
場所＝大田区羽田空港
モノレール整備場駅そば○ターミナルビル、飛行機整備工
場等、周辺の空港関連施設に熱供給する地域冷暖房施設
（旧）○冷水、高温水発生器を内蔵する巨大なヴォリューム
○屋上にはむきだしの大型クーリングタワーがある○壁面の
パイプラインにより他の施設と結ばれる

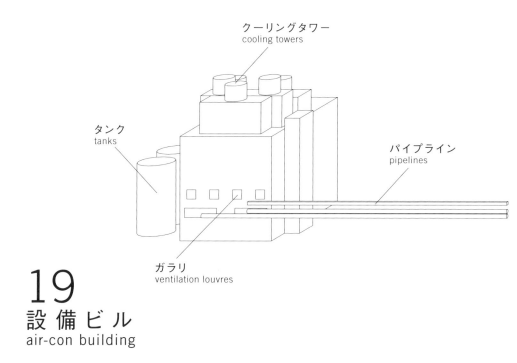

クーリングタワー
cooling towers

タンク
tanks

パイプライン
pipelines

ガラリ
ventilation louvres

19
設備ビル
air-con building

function: district cooling and heating plant
site: Haneda-kuko, Ota-ku
- near the monorail stop called 'Haneda Airport Maintenance Area Station'
- facility for heating and cooling the surrounding buildings related
to the airport, such as aeroplane maintenance factories
- a huge volume made up of mechanical equipment for cooling and heating exchange
- large, open cooling towers on the roof terrace
- pipelines extend from the building to connect into surrounding buildings

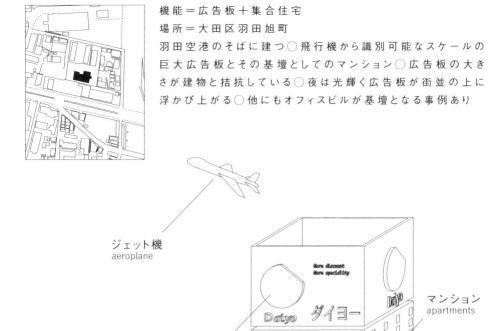

機能＝広告板＋集合住宅
場所＝大田区羽田旭町
羽田空港のそばに建つ○飛行機から識別可能なスケールの
巨大広告板とその基壇としてのマンション○広告板の大き
さが建物と拮抗している○夜は光輝く広告板が街並の上に
浮かび上がる○他にもオフィスビルが基壇となる事例あり

ジェット機
aeroplane

看板
billboard

マンション
apartments

20
広告マンション
billboard apartment house

function: billboard + apartment house
site: Haneda-asahicho, Ota-ku
- stands near Haneda airport
- the scale of the huge billboard suits the view from the aeroplane;
the apartments' role is to hold up this billboard
- the billboard and the building below are almost the same size
- the billboard is almost half again the size of the building below
- in the evening, the flashing neon sign floats above the rest of the city
- sometimes, this kind of billboard is held up by office buildings

機能＝神社＋店舗
場所＝大田区田園調布
東横線・目蒲線多摩川園駅近く○神社の境内の一部が人工
地盤になっている○人工地盤の下は貸店舗、上は境内と駐車
場○類例として飲食店舗の上に神社がのったもの（台東区根
岸）がある

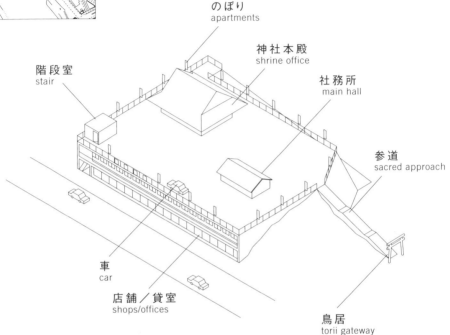

のぼり
apartments

神社本殿
shrine office

社務所
main hall

階段室
stair

参道
sacred approach

車
car

店舗／貸室
shops/offices

鳥居
torii gateway

21
神社ビル
shrine building

function: shrine + shops / offices
site: Denen-chofu, Ota-ku
- near Tamagawaen station, Toyoko and Mekama lines
- the shrine precinct is an artificial ground on a rooftop
- the lower levels contain rented commercial space,
 on the rooftop is the shrine, and carparking
- a similar example of shrine over a restaurant building is in Negishi, Taito-ku

機能＝オフィス＋社宅＋資材置場＋車庫
場所＝世田谷区玉堤
多摩堤通り沿い○土工事会社の事務所と社宅がピロ
ティの上に浮かぶ○グランドレベルは資材（土）置場、
車庫として敷地全面を利用

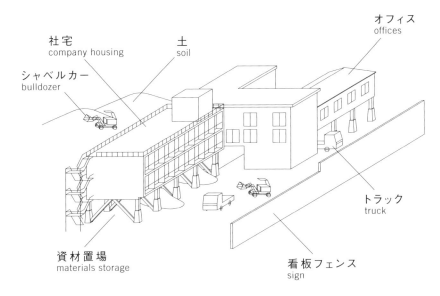

社宅
company housing

土
soil

シャベルカー
bulldozer

オフィス
offices

トラック
truck

資材置場
materials storage

看板フェンス
sign

22
残土アパート
sand apartment house

function: office + company housing
+ building materials storage + truck parking
site: Tamazutsumi, Setagaya-ku
- stands alongside the Tamazutsumi road, and the wide bank of the Tama River
- company housing and office of the earthworks
construction company floats above, on piloti
- the full extent of the ground level of the site is free to be used
for building materials and soil storage, truck parking and so on

機能＝オフィス＋車庫＋倉庫
場所＝杉並区和泉
井の頭線沿い○宅配便の配送センター○スロープの
車路が建物のヴォリュームの中で折り返して出入りする
○ル・コルビュジエのカーペンターセンターを彷彿とさ
せる

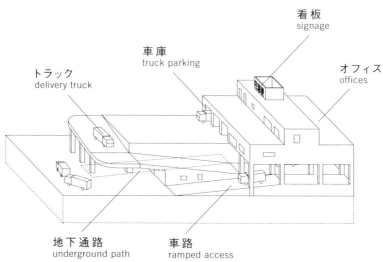

看板
signage

車庫
truck parking

オフィス
offices

トラック
delivery truck

地下通路
underground path

車路
ramped access

23
配送スパイラル
delivery spiral

function: office + truck parking + courier storage centre
site: Izumi, Suginami-ku
- alongside Inokashira railway line
- delivery centre for courier mail
- vehicular ramps fold in and out, through the volume of the building
- it reminds us of Le Corbusiers Carpenter Center

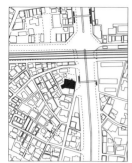

機能＝銭湯＋サウナ＋コインランドリー＋
コンビニエンスストア＋住居
場所＝杉並区高円寺南
環七通り沿い○通り側１階にコンビニとコインランドリー、２
階に銭湯、３階にサウナ○入浴、洗濯、買い物という一連の
行為をひとつの建物にパッケージ○単身者の夜の社交場

住宅
owner's residence

ネオンサイン
neon sign

サウナ
sauna

銭湯
public baths

コンビニ
convenience store

コインランドリー
coin laundry

24
銭湯ツアービル
bath tour building

function: public bath + sauna + coin laundry
+ convenience store + owner's residence
site: Koenji-minami, Suginami-ku
- directly faces the busy Kannana (seventh) traffic ring road
- on the first floor linking to the street is a 24 hour convenience store and coin laundry,
on the second floor is the public bath facility and on the third floor is the sauna
- a package of activity, comprising a sequence of bathing, washing, shopping
- a singles' night spot

機能＝整備工場＋オフィス＋車庫＋仮眠所
場所＝武蔵野市吉祥寺南町
井の頭通り沿いに建つタクシー会社の社屋○元NISSAN
整備工場○1階に整備工場、2階に事務所と車庫、3階に
運転手の仮眠所○人車同床

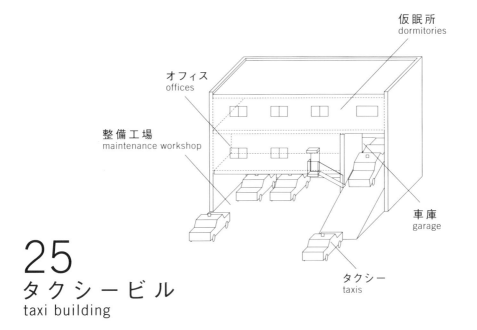

仮眠所
dormitories

オフィス
offices

整備工場
maintenance workshop

車庫
garage

タクシー
taxis

25
タクシービル
taxi building

function: maintenance workshop + office + garage + dormitory
site: Kichijoji-minamicho, Musashino-shi
- the taxi company building stands alongside Inokashira Street
- the building used to be the Nissan repair factory
- on the first floor is the maintenance workshop, on the second floor is the taxi office
and parking, on the third floor is the temporary sleeping area for the drivers
- humans and cars are sleeping next to each other

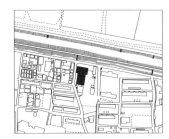

機能＝整備工場＋オフィス＋車庫
場所＝板橋区舟渡
荒川堤防沿い○1階に整備工場、2階、3階に事務所、
2階〜6階に車庫○トラック用なのでカータワーより階
高が高い

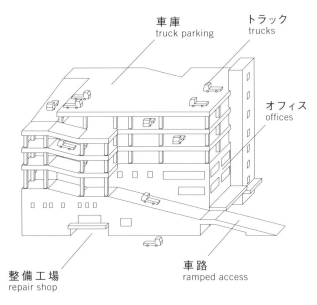

車庫
truck parking

トラック
trucks

オフィス
offices

整備工場
repair shop

車路
ramped access

26
トラックタワー
truck tower

function: repair shop + office + truck parking
site: Funado, Itabashi-ku
- stands alongside the Arakawa River embankment
- on the first floor is the repair shop, on the second and third floors
are offices and from the second to the sixth floors is truck parking
- because the parking is for trucks, the floor
to ceiling heights are larger than for a 'car tower'

機能＝高速道路インターチェンジ＋テニスコート
場所＝足立区西加平
環七と交差する首都高加平ランプにふたつある螺旋スロープのうちの一方○車路に取り囲まれた中庭がテニスコートになっている○もう一方の中庭は道路公団パトカー車庫○外観は擬石ブロックのルスティカ風○鋼製列柱回廊の中庭はバロック風

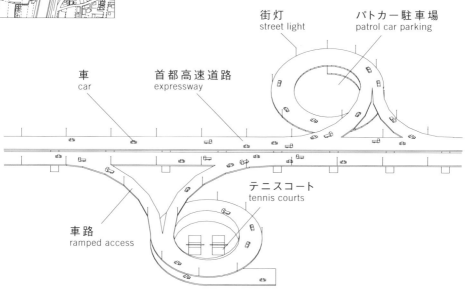

街灯
street light

パトカー駐車場
patrol car parking

車
car

首都高速道路
expressway

テニスコート
tennis courts

車路
ramped access

27
インターコート
interchange court

function: repair shop + office + truck parking
site: Nishikahei, Adachi-ku
- one of the interchange spirals at Kahei,
which links the expressway with the Kannana (seventh) traffic ring road
- the courtyard enclosed by the spiralling ramp has become tennis courts
- the courtyard on the other side is car parking for the expressway patrol cars
- the ramp is enclosed below with an external fake stone block facade,
in an rustic style
- an iron colonnde surrounds the courtyard, in an baroque style

機能＝ガソリンスタンド（１、２Ｆ）＋オフィス
場所＝新宿区西新宿
パークタワーの近くの立体交差点に建つ○上下に交叉する
道路それぞれに接するふたつのＧＳの積層○同じ石油会社
だが１Ｆと２Ｆで営業時間がちがう

看板
signage

２Ｆ ガソリンスタンド
higher petrol station

オフィス
offices

１Ｆ ガソリンスタンド
lower petrol station

陸橋
bridging road

28
ＧＳデュプレックス
double layer petrol station

function: petrol station + office
site: Nishishinjuku, Shinjuku-ku
- at a split intersection near Park Tower Hotel
- double layer petrol stations can be accessed
from both the lower and higher roadways
- although they are run by the same petroleum company,
the 2 stations have differing operating times

機能＝スーパーマーケット＋自動車教習所
場所＝葛飾区金町
2層のスーパーマーケット屋上に自動車教習所が積層○買収未了の敷地建物を包含○カーブする引込線に縁取られた敷地形状をそのままヴォリューム化○坂道発進練習用スロープの下に外部へのスロープ出入口あり

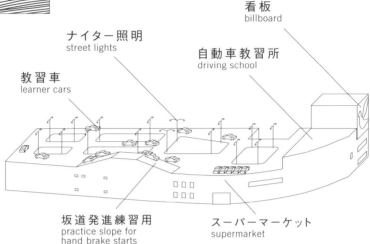

看板
billboard

ナイター照明
street lights

自動車教習所
driving school

教習車
learner cars

坂道発進練習用
practice slope for
hand brake starts

スーパーマーケット
supermarket

29
スーパー・カー・スクール
super car school

function: supermarket + driving school
site: Kanamachi, Katsusika-ku
- on top of the double layer supermarket lands a layer of driving school
- the site includes parcels of other people's property which could not be purchased
- the condition of the site, framed by the curve of the railroad,
is expressed directly in the extruded volume of the building
- the entry ramp is framed above by the practice slopes for hand brake starts

機能＝下水処理施設＋球技場
場所＝新宿区上落合
首都高葛西ジャンクションそば○葛西下水処理場の上部を
球技場として利用○野球４面　サッカー・ラグビー１面○ナイ
ター照明あり○においあり○葛西に類例あり

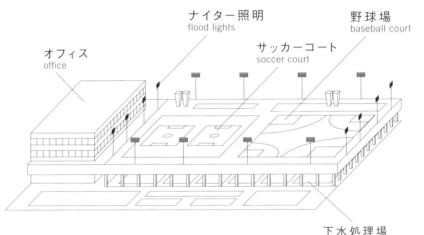

オフィス
office

ナイター照明
flood lights

サッカーコート
soccer court

野球場
baseball court

下水処理場
sewage disposal plant

30
下水コート
sewage courts

function: sewage disposal plant + sporting facilities
site: Kamiochiai, Shinjuku-ku
- near the Kasai expressway junction
- the top of the Kasai sewage disposal plant is utilised for sports playing
- 4 baseball courts, 1 soccer court, 1 rugby court
- flood lights for night games
- scent of sewage
- another similar example in kasai

機能＝貯水池＋球場
場所＝江東区亀戸
亀戸天神そば○横十間川ぞいの水道局、120ｍ正方形平
面の貯水池上に野球場、テニスコートが積層○隣接する公
団団地の中庭のようにみえる

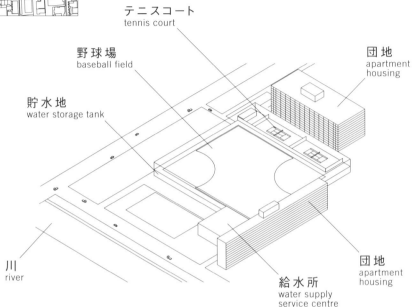

テニスコート
tennis court

野球場
baseball field

団地
apartment
housing

貯水地
water storage tank

川
river

給水所
water supply
service centre

団地
apartment
housing

31
上水コート
supply water courts

function: water treatment plant + sporting facilities
site: Kameido, Koto-ku
- near Kameido Shrine
- water treatment plant along Yokojukken river
-120 sqm surface area of water storage tank covered
by a baseball field and tennis courts
- appears to be a courtyard for the surrounding housing blocks

機能＝墓地十道路
場所＝渋谷区千駄ヶ谷
キラー通りとスタジアム通りの交差点付近○墓地の下
を道路がくぐる○別名「お化けトンネル」○故・池田貴
族の霊感スポット

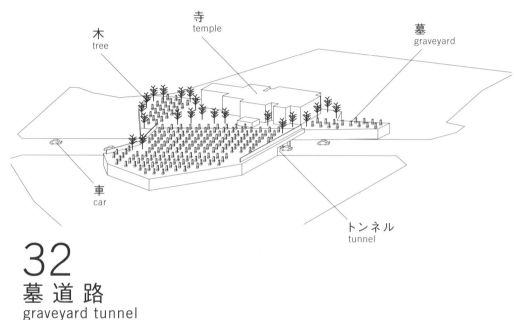

木
tree

寺
temple

墓
graveyard

車
car

トンネル
tunnel

32
墓道路
graveyard tunnel

function: graveyard + road
site: Sendagaya, Shibuya-ku
- around the area of the crossing of Killer street and Stadium street
- the road slices under the temple graveyard
- nicknamed 'ghost tunnel'
- the medium Kizoku Ikeda has named this a psychic spot

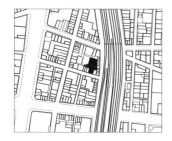

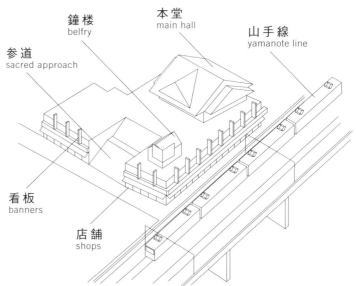

参道
sacred approach

鐘楼
belfry

本堂
main hall

山手線
yamanote line

看板
banners

店舗
shops

33
アメ横空中寺
ameyoko flying temple

function: temple + shops
site: Ueno,Taito-ku
- the block faces Ameyoko shopping street
and flies alongside the raised Yamanote train line
- the shrine precinct is established on artificial ground held up
by part of the Ameyoko shopping area
- the belfry is wrapped in signboards
- temple banners double as shop signage
- stalls traditionallly aligning the sacred approach wind under the shrine precinct

機能＝デパート＋映画館＋公園
場所＝台東区上野公園
山の手線上野駅そば○上野の山を押さえるおよそ１３０ｍの
建築擁壁○上野公園に連続する屋上に西郷隆盛像

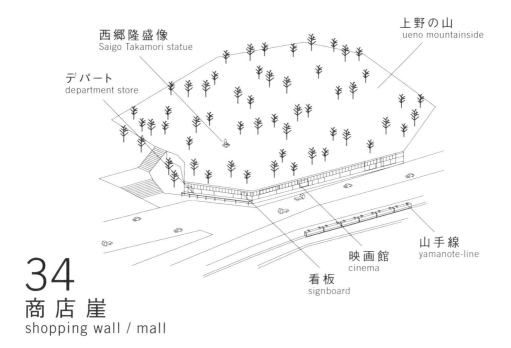

西郷隆盛像
Saigo Takamori statue

上野の山
ueno mountainside

デパート
department store

看板
signboard

映画館
cinema

山手線
yamanote-line

34
商店崖
shopping wall / mall

function: shops + cinema + park
site: Uenopark, Taito-ku
- near Ueno station on the Yamanote line
- 130m of architectural retaining wall holding back Ueno mountainside
- a statue of Takamori Saigo on the rooftop cum Ueno park ground

機能＝博物館＋駅
場所＝墨田区東向島
東武伊勢崎線東向島駅下にある東武鉄道交通博物館○リ
ニアな形態は鉄道車両の展示に最適○ホームの下にある
窓から本物の線路を観る展示あり

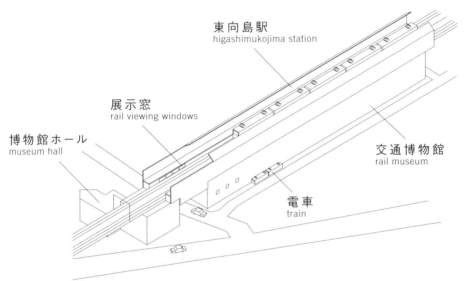

東向島駅
higashimukojima station

展示窓
rail viewing windows

博物館ホール
museum hall

交通博物館
rail museum

電車
train

35
レールミュージーアム
rail museum

function: rail museum + rail station
site: Higashimukojima, Sumida-ku
- museum of Tobu railway lines under Higashimukojima station of the Tobu Isezaki line
- the linear form of the site is ideally suited to display the length of each carriage
- windows underneath the platform-in-use show a close up view of the rails themselves

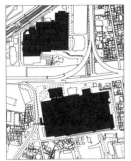

機能＝下水処理施設＋公園
場所＝葛飾区小菅
首都高小菅ジャンクションそば ○ 下水処理場を首都高と川
が分断 ○ 一方はカーブする首都高にあわせて雁行したヴォ
リューム ○ 屋上はテニスコート5面、池を含む日本庭園あり
○ においなし

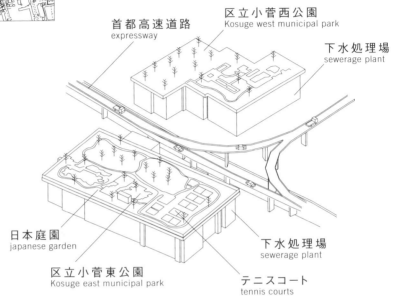

首都高速道路
expressway

区立小菅西公園
Kosuge west municipal park

下水処理場
sewerage plant

日本庭園
japanese garden

区立小菅東公園
Kosuge east municipal park

下水処理場
sewerage plant

テニスコート
tennis courts

36
ツイン下水御苑
twin deluxe sewerage gardens

function: park gardens + sewerage plant
site: Kosuge, Katsushika-ku
- near the metropolitan expressways' Kosuge junction
- the expressway route and river divide the plant into 2 parts
- one side adjusts to the curve of the expressway corner by its zig zag form
- the roof terrace houses 5 tennis courts
and a traditional japanese garden, including a small lake
- no sense of sewage

機能＝プール＋レストラン＋ゲームセンター＋
ホール＋駐車場
場所＝足立区西新井
東京マリン○住宅街の巨大プール○1階はゲームセンター、
駐車場、レストラン、その屋上にプールと植栽された庭○ス
ライダーはさらなる刺激を求めて年々増築中

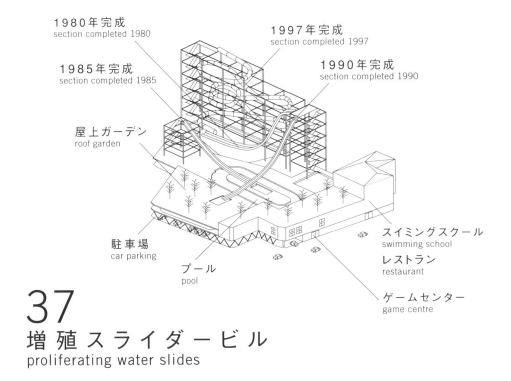

1980年完成
section completed 1980

1997年完成
section completed 1997

1985年完成
section completed 1985

1990年完成
section completed 1990

屋上ガーデン
roof garden

駐車場
car parking

プール
pool

スイミングスクール
swimming school

レストラン
restaurant

ゲームセンター
game centre

37
増殖スライダービル
proliferating water slides

function: play pools + restaurant + game centre + hall + parking
site: Nishiarai, Adachi-ku
- "Tokyo Marine"
- the enormous pool towers over the residential area
- the ground floor contains game centre, car parking and restaurant,
the roof terrace contains pool facilities and planted garden
- the growing number of slides are becoming more and more sensational each year

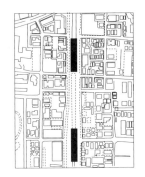

機能＝トンネル換気塔
場所＝杉並区井草
環八井萩トンネルそば○西武新宿線を挟んで向かい合う環
八中央のふたつの巨大な換気塔○機械室、管理室、事務
室の付属ヴォリュームあり○パリ・ヴァンドーム広場のオベ
リスクに対抗？した環八の新アイストップ

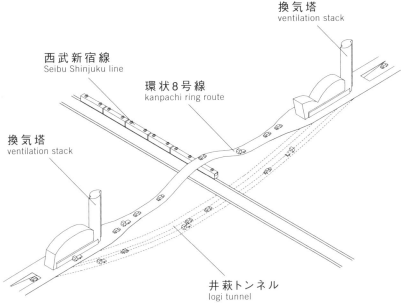

換気塔
ventilation stack

西武新宿線
Seibu Shinjuku line

環状8号線
kanpachi ring route

換気塔
ventilation stack

井萩トンネル
Iogi tunnel

38
換気オベリスク
ventilator obelisk

function: tunnel ventilation
site: Igusa, Suginami-ku
- attached to Kanpachi-Iogi tunnel
- the obelisk-stacks face each other across the Seibu Shinjuku line,
and stand resolutely in the middle of traffic
- machine rooms and offices are linked to each obelisk
- a new kind of landmark rivalling the obelisk of Vendome Place in Paris

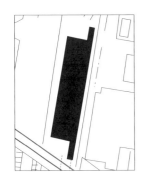

機能＝駅＋集合住宅＋車庫
場所＝松戸市幸谷
私鉄流山駅幸谷駅と坂川に挟まれて建つ○Ｌ字型の集合
住宅１階のバルコニーが駅のホーム○隣接する１階部分は
タクシーの車庫○坂川護岸歩道はマンションのエントランス
に連続

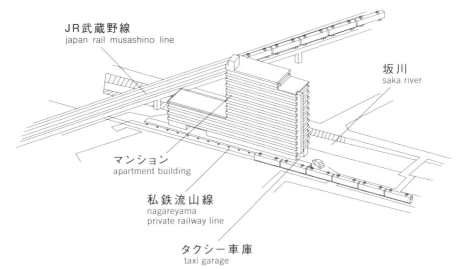

JR武蔵野線
japan rail musashino line

坂川
saka river

マンション
apartment building

私鉄流山線
nagareyama
private railway line

タクシー車庫
taxi garage

39
駅のホーム
apartment station

function: train station + apartments + taxi garage
site: Koya, Matsudo-shi
- sandwiched in between Koya station of the Nagareyama line and Saka River
- the housing forms an L-shaped section,
the train station platform appears as the ground floor balcony
- the ground floor is a garage for taxis
- the concrete promenade to the river is continuous with the building's entry

機能＝鉄道十集合住宅
場所＝八王子市東浅川町
京王線高尾駅近くの高架下 ◯ 私鉄の社員寮として利用 ◯ 住戸数43戸、総延長約300ｍ ◯ 橋脚のスパンに規格化された住戸ヴォリュームが挿入される

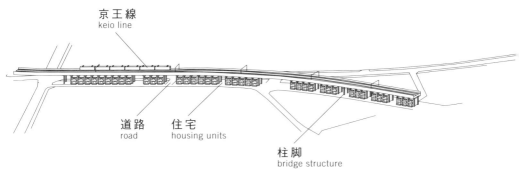

京王線
keio line

道路
road

住宅
housing units

柱脚
bridge structure

40
ムカデ住宅
centipede housing

function: railway + housing units
site: Higashiasakawa-cho, Hachioji-shi
- underneath raised railway structure near Takao station, Keio line
- utilised as Keio company housing
- 43 housing units over approximately 300 metres length
- the housing unit volumes are inserted to match the structural span

機能＝車検＋整備販売＋保険＋
塗装＋板金＋公営駐車場＋住宅
場所＝板橋区大山金井町
首都高が上を走る中仙道沿い○ターンテーブルを自動車関連
の様々な職種の建物が囲む○パーキングタワーのファサードは
代理店のメッセージが流れる電光掲示板○車コミュニティー

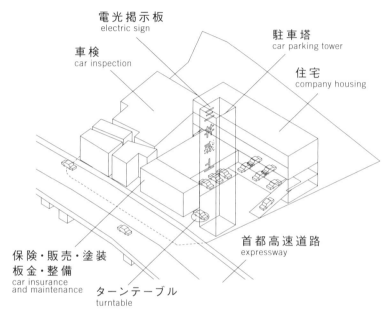

電光掲示板
electric sign

駐車塔
car parking tower

車検
car inspection

住宅
company housing

保険・販売・塗装
板金・整備
car insurance
and maintenance

ターンテーブル
turntable

首都高速道路
expressway

41
自動車ビレッジ
vehicular village

function: car inspection + maintenance + show room +
insurance + public parking + company housing
site: Ooyamakanaimachi, Itabashi-ku
- alongside Nakasendo road and the expressway overhead
- the various buildings of the village gather around the turntable courtyard
- the tower runs an electric message from the showroom down the facade
- auto community

機能＝ダイビングスクール
場所＝荒川区南千住
隅田川沿い、常磐線から見える○水槽の螺旋階段付青い筒に教室や倉庫の箱がドッキング○水槽の丸い明かり窓から街を眺める○頂部の潜水ヘルメットがアクセント○潜水機会社経営

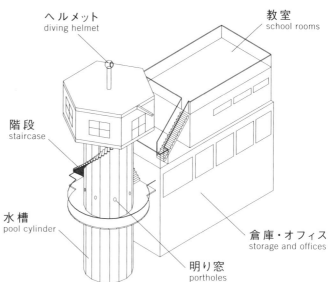

ヘルメット
diving helmet

教室
school rooms

階段
staircase

水槽
pool cylinder

倉庫・オフィス
storage and offices

明り窓
portholes

42
ダイビングタワー
diving tower

function: diving school
site: Minamisenju, Arakawa-ku
- alongside Sumida River, visible from the Joban railway line
- a staircase spirals around the blue cylinder tower pool
and docks into the school rooms and storage block
- portholes for looking out towards the city
- a diving helmet is raised as a pinnacle for the tower
- management by diving tank producing company

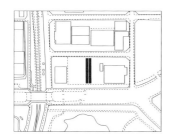

機能＝立体コンテナ置き場
場所＝大田区東海
都立東京港野鳥公園前○トラックのシャーシーが１０層
に積みあがり立体的に格納される○シャーシーを列ごと
に色分け○高層化して得られた残余空間を駐車場とし
て利用

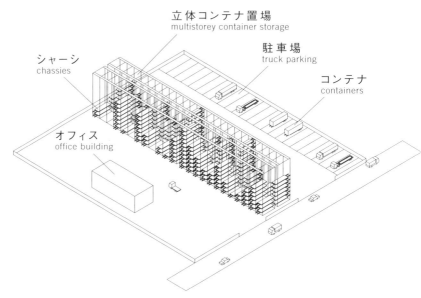

シャーシ
chassies

オフィス
office building

立体コンテナ置場
multistorey container storage

駐車場
truck parking

コンテナ
containers

43
シャーシーマンション
chassis apartments

function: multistorey chassis storage + truck parking
site: Tokai, Ota-ku
- in front of the municipal Tokyo Bay wild bird sanctuary
- truck chassies are layered 10 levels high to be packed into a solid block
- chassies are colour coded in rows
- the ground space gained by raising
the containers is utilised for truck parking

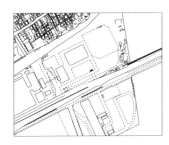

機能＝オフィス
場所＝川崎市鶴見区生麦
産業道路鶴見大橋そば○コンテナ置き場入り口に積まれた4つのコンテナからなる事務所○青いボディに斜体で書かれたトリコロールのタイポグラフィが目印○コンテナ、アルミサッシ、鉄骨階段、アンテナ、太陽熱パネル、電線の突然の出会い

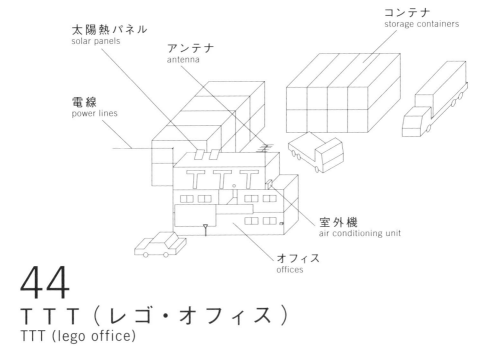

太陽熱パネル
solar panels

アンテナ
antenna

コンテナ
storage containers

電線
power lines

室外機
air conditioning unit

オフィス
offices

44
ＴＴＴ（レゴ・オフィス）
TTT (lego office)

function: container offices + container stockyard
site: Namamugi, Tsurumi-ku, Kawasaki
- near Tsurumi Ohashi bridge, Sangyo road
- office building made up of 4 containers stacked at the entry of the container yard
- coloured italic text on a blue container body makes
a tricolore identity for the company
- unexpected coming together of storage containers,
aluminium sashes, steel stairs, antennas, solar panels, power lines

TTT

安全第一 ✚

TEL. 045 510 2500
FAX. 045 510 2475

TANEY (TOKYO)
TANK TERMINAL

機能＝上越新幹線＋神社
場所＝北区赤羽台
埼京線・東北・上越新幹線赤羽駅近く○神社の境内下がト
ンネル○さらにその背後には私立小中高校○新幹線と平行
にスロープの参道○新幹線通勤により知らぬ間のお百度参
りも可

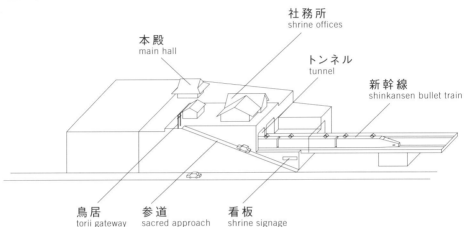

本殿
main hall

社務所
shrine offices

トンネル
tunnel

新幹線
shinkansen bullet train

鳥居
torii gateway

参道
sacred approach

看板
shrine signage

45
トンネル神社
tunnel shrine

function: shinkansen + shrine
site: Akabanedai, Kita-ku
- near Akabane station of Saikyo and Shinkansen lines
- tunnel under the shrine precinct
- further into the hillside is a private primary and middle school
- the sacred approach slopes parrallel to the Shinkansen route
- Shinkansen commuters have the opportunity to make daily prayers without realising it

機能＝寺＋集合住宅
場所＝横浜市保土ヶ谷区台町
東横線反町駅そば○金比羅神社が隣接○マンションの内
部階段と屋上ブリッジが参道○玉砂利ならぬ防水シート仕
上げの屋上が前庭○シンメトリーに並ぶ鳩小屋は境内の灯
篭のよう

山
moutainside

ブリッジ
bridge

マンション屋上
apartment roof terrace
(temple forecourt)

寺
temple

内部階段
internal staircase
(sacred approach)

ピロティ
piloti

マンション
apartment block

駐車場
car parking

46
マンション山寺
apartment mountain temple

function: buddhist temple + private appartment housing
site: Daimachi, Hodogaya-ku, Yokohama-shi
- near Tanmachi station of Toyoko train line
- Konpira shrine is adjacent
- the religious approach passes the internal staircase of the housing,
across the apartment roof and bridge to the main temple hall
- the forecourt of the temple is not pebbles or gravel, but the waterproof sheeting of the
apartment roof terrace
- ventilators aligned in parallel on the roof terrace are like lanterns

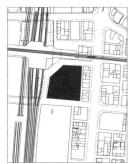

機能＝駅前広場＋献血ルーム
場所＝千代田区外神田
秋葉原駅前○秋葉原のネオンビルに囲まれた、3on3やスケートボードなどのタウンスポーツの広場○広場にさりげなく置かれた献血ルームには広場側と道路側の両側に入り口あり○若くて生きのいい血求む

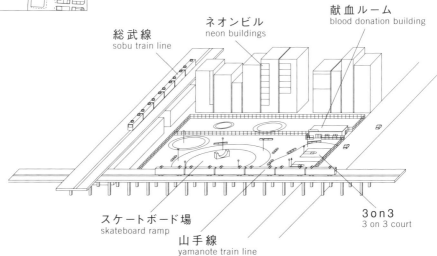

総武線
sobu train line

ネオンビル
neon buildings

献血ルーム
blood donation building

スケートボード場
skateboard ramp

山手線
yamanote train line

3on3
3 on 3 court

47
吸血公園
vampire park

function: public square + blood donation
site: Sotokanda, Chiyoda-ku
- in front of Akihabara station
- neon buildings of Akihabara surround open space containing urban sports
such as skateboard ramps and 3 on 3 courts
- the blood donation building sits innocently in the square
with entries to both the square and the street
- desire for young and fresh blood

機能＝クレーン会社社屋
場所＝横浜市南区平田町
国道1号線沿い○タワークレーン会社のクレーン倉庫
兼社屋○カラフルなトラスフレームが鉄骨の棚に積ま
れる○不況でタワークレーンの出番減少中

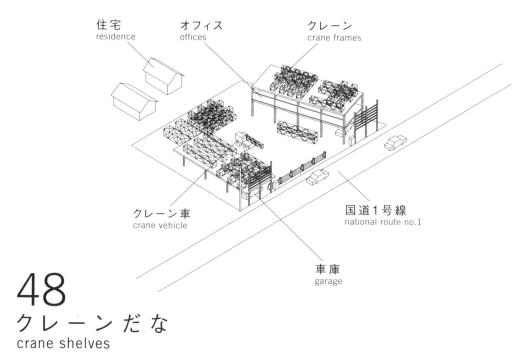

住宅
residence

オフィス
offices

クレーン
crane frames

クレーン車
crane vehicle

国道1号線
national route no.1

車庫
garage

48
クレーンだな
crane shelves

function: crane company office building
site: Hiratamachi, Minami-ku, Yokohama-shi
- alongside National Route no.1
- crane storage and office facilities for crane company
- colourful truss frames are stacked on steel shelves

機能＝旧貨物線高架＋左官工場

場所＝千代田区飯田橋

貨物線旧飯田町駅への引き込み高架下の左官工事会社○
貨物線廃止後の高架上部に社屋を増築○前面道路のアス
ファルトが連続する高架下の各スパンに土、砂、砂利、石な
どの骨材を貯蔵○弓なりの建物の中央を道路が横断

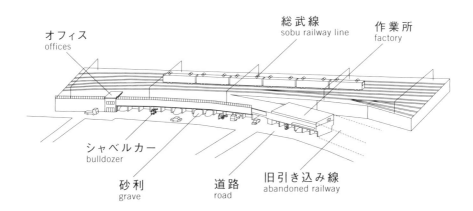

オフィス
offices

総武線
sobu railway line

作業所
factory

シャベルカー
bulldozer

砂利
grave

道路
road

旧引き込み線
abandoned railway

49
ユーレイ・ル・ファクトリー
ghost rail factory

function: abandoned railway + plaster factory
site: Iidamachi, Chiyoda-ku
- plaster factory under the structure of the disused branch line
for the old freight train to Iidamachi station
- following the discontinuation of the freight line, the company
has extended by building the factory on top of the rail track space
- the structural span makes pockets for storing earth, sand,
gravel, stones etc, facing directly onto the asphalt road
- a road cuts through the bow shaped building

機能＝マンション＋擁壁
場所＝川崎市麻生区細江
小田急線読売ランド駅そば○削った山を押さえる擁壁と建物がクロス梁で結ばれて構造的に連続○擁壁が山を押さえ、建物が擁壁を押さえる力学連鎖○建物の外部廊下はペンキを塗られることで土木構造物から差異化○建物と擁壁の間に無数の梁が交錯する外部空間が出現

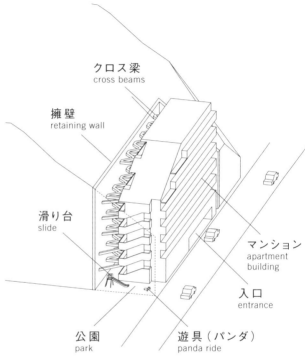

クロス梁
cross beams

擁壁
retaining wall

滑り台
slide

マンション
apartment building

入口
entrance

公園
park

遊具（パンダ）
panda ride

50
擁壁マンション
retaining wall apartments

function: apartment building + retaining wall
site: Hosoe, Asou-ku, Kawasaki-shi
- near Yomiuri Land station of Odakyu railway line
- the retaining wall and the apartment building
become one through the criss-crossing structure
- the wall holding back the mountain joins forces with the weight of the building
- an attempt to separate architecture and engineering
by painting the external balcony but not the criss-cross structure
- a strange space filled with crossing structure appears

機能＝公園＋高架道路＋養護施設
場所＝港区南青山
青山墓地に挟まれた、麻布の谷と六本木の台地の段差に
かかる青山橋の下○コルビュジエ風カラーリングの高架の
柱脚を利用したモダニズム風の建物の養護施設○隣接す
る区立の児童遊園や青山墓地は屋敷森○都心とは思えな
い静けさと緑豊かな風景を独占

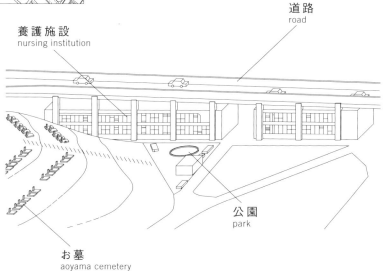

養護施設
nursing institution

道路
road

公園
park

お墓
aoyama cemetery

51
ブリッジハウス
bridge home

function: children's home + park + raised roadway
site: Minami-aoyama, Minato-ku
- under the Aoyama bridge which spans over the valley of Aoyama cemetery
- modern architecture of Corbusian colours makes use of bridge structure as piloti
- Aoyama cemetery and the park neighbouring the home are like grounds to an estate
- the home monopolises this serenity and abundant greenery
which seems unthinkable in the middle of the metropolis

機能＝農家＋畑＋野菜販売キオスク
場所＝練馬区早宮
スプロール化で歯抜け状に農地が宅地化された住宅地
○周囲を住宅地に囲まれた畑の道路側のキオスクで畑
で捕れた新鮮野菜を安価で販売○キオスクの奥に農家
の母屋あり畦道のアプローチでつながれる○輸送費ゼ
ロの超ショートサイクル経済学○畑の端に御先祖のお
墓あり

農家母屋
farmhouse

納屋
storage

ビニールハウス
green house

野菜販売所
vegetable stall

畑
fields

先祖の墓
ancestral grave

52
宅 地 農 場
residential farm

function: farmhouse + fields + vegetable stall
site: Hayamiya, Nerima-ku
- a suburbia developed in random pockets of farming land
- on the road side of the fields is a stall selling
fresh vegetables direct to the customer at low prices
- the farmhouse and stall are connected by a thin foot path through the fields
- a super-shortcut economic cycle needs zero transportation time or cost
- the tradition of the ancestor's grave in the corner of the fields
is retained despite surrounding residential development
- the ultimate situation for the direct sale of produce

機能＝宅配便ターミナル
場所＝埼玉県新座市
○ 関越自動車道練馬料金所脇 ○ 関越を走り抜ける大形トラックから小型トラックへ積み換えるターミナル ○ 1階：宅急便の仕分け用荷物プール、2階：事務所、屋上：トラック駐車場 ○ 大音響で流れるヒットソングのリズムにのってベルトコンベアーで運ばれる荷物

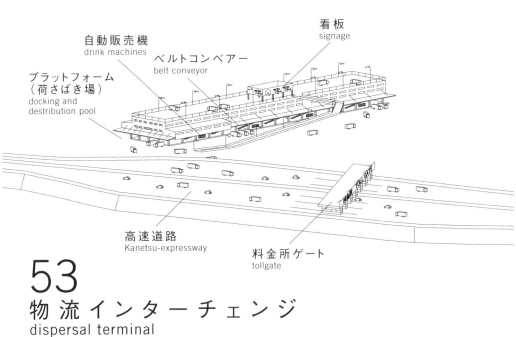

自動販売機
drink machines

ベルトコンベアー
belt conveyor

看板
signage

プラットフォーム
（荷さばき場）
docking and
destribution pool

高速道路
Kanetsu-expressway

料金所ゲート
tollgate

53
物流インターチェンジ
dispersal terminal

function: courier station
site: Niizashi, Saitama-ken
- next to the Nerima tollgate of the Kanetsu expressway
- a station for transfering large packages
on large trucks into small packages on small trucks
- ground floor docking and transfer pool,
middle floors administration, rooftop truck parking
- packages conveyed around the transfer pool,
riding on the rhythm of radio hit stations

機能＝駐車場＋マンション＋
ファミリーレストラン＋ゴルフ練習場
場所＝板橋区桜川
川越街道沿い、ゴルフ練習場の建て替え○1階：駐車場、
2階：ファミリーレストラン、ゴルフ練習場、3階：ゴルフ練
習場、住宅○レストラン、ゴルフ練習場つきマンション○ネ
ットがあるので大事にはいたらないがゴルフボールが廊下を
直撃、○お父さんのウィークエンド・ライフのパッケージ

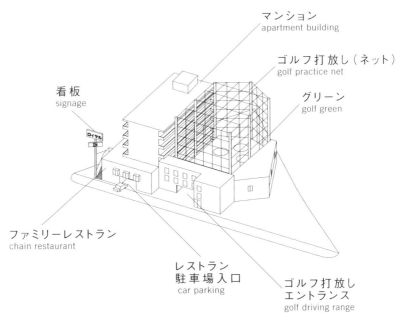

マンション
apartment building

ゴルフ打放し（ネット）
golf practice net

グリーン
golf green

看板
signage

ファミリーレストラン
chain restaurant

レストラン
駐車場入口
car parking

ゴルフ打放し
エントランス
golf driving range

54
ロイヤルゴルフマンション
royal golf apartments

function: 'royal host' chain restaurant +
golf practice range + apartment building + car parking
site: Sakuragawa, Itabashi-ku
- next to Kawagoe road, previously a ground level golf practice range only
- ground floor car parking, middle floors 'royal host'
and golf practice range, upper floors apartments
- housing with the benefit of a spacious netted forecourt and optional restaurant
- a tathes, weekend package is available inside metropolitan Tokyo
- beautiful view through the nets of the golf practice range from the external corridors

機能＝立体駐車場＋レストラン
場所＝中央区銀座
松屋通りぞい「東京駐車ビル」○１、２階にレストラン、１階に
ターンテーブルのある駐車場への入口あり○高い地価のため
車路を節約○中央の車両用エレベーターは回転しながら上昇
し各階で車を方射する○コンクリート造の白いフレームとアル
ミのフレームでオフィスビルに擬装

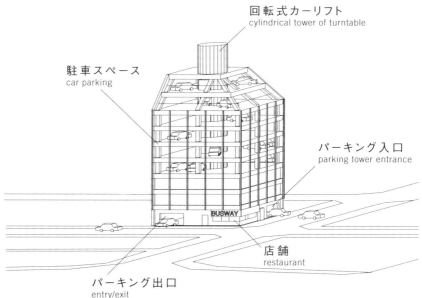

回転式カーリフト
cylindrical tower of turntable

駐車スペース
car parking

パーキング入口
parking tower entrance

パーキング出口
entry/exit

店舗
restaurant

55
カーオフィス
car parking office

function: parking tower + restaurant
site: Ginza, Chuo-ku
- the original 'Tokyo parking building' faces Matsuya street
- the lower 2 floors are utilised by restaurants except
for the carpark entry leading to a turntable tower
- due to the extremely high price of land in Ginza,
there is no chance to waste space on circulation ramps
- the pure white concrete and alminium frames show off the cars inside
- the revolving lift is a highlight
- the final possible extent of the mechanisation of architecture, before the machine
completely takes over, as in more contemporary parking towers

機能＝立体駐車場＋庭

場所＝品川区西品川

造園業者の庭と立体駐車場がスーパーインポーズ○駐車場のグレージングスラブは庭の輪郭に追随○庭木がグレージングの床を貫通して屋上に飛び出す○1階は自動車と苗木、造園工作機が共存○入口スロープ脇が自販機で固められる。パーク＆ドリンク。○隣に社屋、社長宅あり

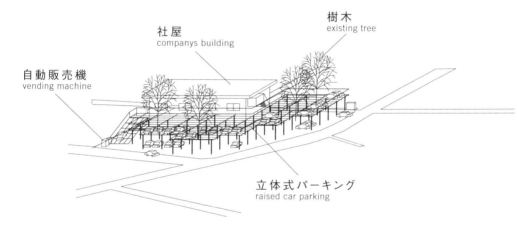

自動販売機
vending machine

社屋
companys building

樹木
existing tree

立体式パーキング
raised car parking

56
グリーンパーキング
green parking

function: multi-layer ramped car parking + garden
site: Nishi Shinagawa, Shinagawa-ku
- headquarters of a landsacape company,
and company president's home beside a carparking building
- because the site used to be a garden, there still remains a stone wall and some trees
- keyaki and persimon trees push up through the grating of the floor above
- a sparse building including much greenery
- drink machines cluster around the ramp entry to encourage taking a break

機能＝修理工場＋店舗＋駐車場＋ボウリング場
場所＝練馬区北町
環八と川越街道の交差点○2階の駐車場に直接ドライブ・
イン○1階は整備工場と店舗、2階駐車場、3〜4階車用
品店舗、5階ゲームセンターとボウリング場○車を整備して
もらう間にボウリングや買物を楽しめる○コンクリート打ち
はなしに黄色い看板、ボウリングの巨大ピンが目印

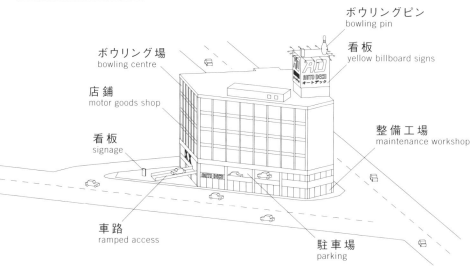

ボウリングピン
bowling pin

看板
yellow billboard signs

ボウリング場
bowling centre

店舗
motor goods shop

整備工場
maintenance workshop

看板
signage

車路
ramped access

駐車場
parking

57
オートデパート
auto department store

function: maintenance workshop + motor goods shop +
store user parking + ten pin bowling
site: Kitamachi, Nerima-ku
- at the corner of Kanpachi ring route and Kawagoe road,
the building volume fills the extent of the site
- direct, drive-in, ramped access to second storey user parking
- car related activities are stacked on top of each other
- yellow billboards over undressed concrete facades,
a huge bowling pin is the crowning sign
- bowling in the spare time created by waiting for car repair work

AUTO TECH
オートテック
創業20周年記念セール
ビックテック
Enjoy Car Life!!
カーナビゲーション
オイル/バッテリー
ワックス/洗車用品
カーアクセサリー
タイヤ/アルミホイール
日本最大級のカー用品専門店
日本最大級の
カー用品専門店
ビックテック
AUTO TECH
AUTO TECH

機能＝ファミリーレストラン＋
スポーツ用品店＋駐車場
場所＝豊島区南長崎
目白通り沿い○３つのファミリーレストランとスポーツ
用品店が人工地盤の上に並ぶ○１階の駐車場は隣
接するゴルフ練習場と共通○和洋中のよりどりみどり

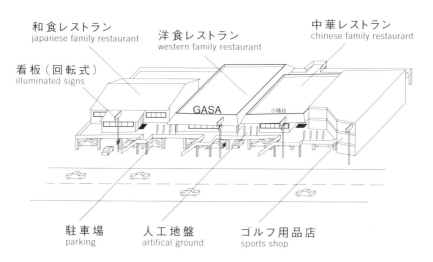

和食レストラン
japanese family restaurant

洋食レストラン
western family restaurant

中華レストラン
chinese family restaurant

看板（回転式）
illuminated signs

GASA

小喰坊

駐車場
parking

人工地盤
artifical ground

ゴルフ用品店
sports shop

58
ファミレス３兄弟
family restaurant triplets

function: family restaurants + sports goods shop + user parking
site: Minaminagasaki, Toshima-ku
- alongside Mejiro road
- 3 restaurant buildings and a sports shop building line up on top of artifical ground
- the ground level parking under the artifical ground and beyond
is shared with the golf practice range on the site behind
- make your choice from Japanese, Western or Chinese cuisine

機能＝青果市場＋店舗
場所＝新宿区北新宿
青果市場の屋上が駐車場○周囲には段ボールやクッションなどの梱包材の店舗が集まる○柱が換気塔を兼ねて、下階にこもった野菜の生臭さを解消○道路が折り畳まれて部分的に巾が広がった流動的な空間

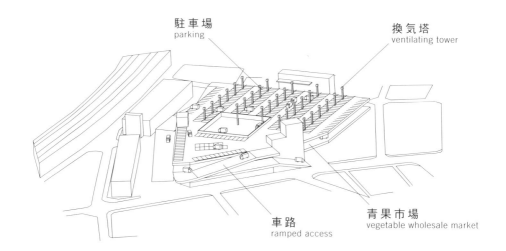

駐車場
parking

換気塔
ventilating tower

車路
ramped access

青果市場
vegetable wholesale market

59
青果タウン
vegetable town

function: vegetable wholesale market + related shops
site: Kitashinjuku, Shinjuku-ku
- the multi level market can be accessed from many different levels and directions
- the roof terrace of the building is market car parking,
and location of loading and initial exchange
- the surrounding area is filled with shops for packaging, boxes and stuffing
- structural columns double as ventilation pipes,
to take away the smells of raw vegetables
- fluid space obtained by the folding and enlargement of the road

機能＝駅＋スーパーマーケット＋店舗
場所＝目黒区大岡山＋大田区北千束
東急目黒線（大井町線）大岡山駅○駅の暗渠化によって
空地となった地上階に建つ軽量な建物○線路（松の木の
根）の上部に1階建ての私鉄系列のスーパーや店舗（松茸）
が並ぶ○類似のビルが東急線沿いに増殖中

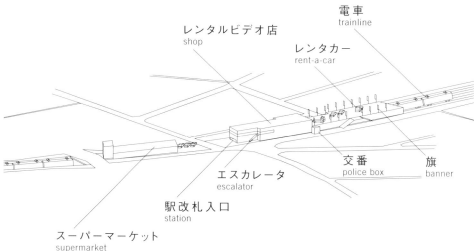

レンタルビデオ店
shop

電車
trainline

レンタカー
rent-a-car

交番
police box

旗
banner

エスカレータ
escalator

駅改札入口
station

スーパーマーケット
supermarket

60
松茸型レールビル
sprouting building

function: train station + supermarket + shops + rent-a-car
site: Ookayama, Meguro-ku + Kitasenzoku, Ota-ku
- rail interchange station of Tokyu Meguro and Oimachi lines
- relocating the station underground makes a vacancy
on the ground floor quickly filled with lightweight building
- the railway line (root) company 'Tokyu' develops
the company owned supermarket and shops (sprouts) above
- similar buildings are sprouting all over the Tokyu railway system

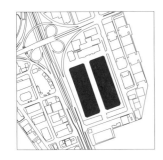

機能＝倉庫＋ターミナル＋駐車場
場所＝大田区平和島
平和島インター前，全長３００ｍ長の巨大ツインビル○中央に倉庫とエレベーター，周囲に車両路がまわる○斜路によるダイナミックなファサードは不同沈下と見間違う迫力○立体化駐車場は今流行の現代建築の元祖？

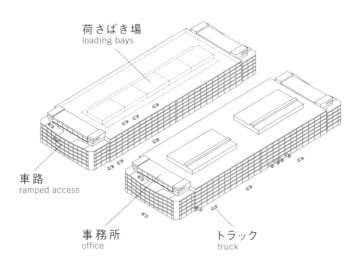

荷さばき場
loading bays

車路
ramped access

事務所
office

トラック
truck

61
TRC（東京流通センター）
tokyo dispersal centre

function: storage station + truck parking
site: Heiwa-jima, Ota-ku
- huge twin buildings each 300 metres long,
stand in front of the Heiwa-jima exit of the expressway
- the centre of each building is filled with storage and elevators,
the rim is ringed with sloping truck circulation
- the end facades are dynamic due to the visible diagonal
of the ramp, and look like differential settlement
- perhaps multi-storey parking is the ancestor of contemporary architecture?

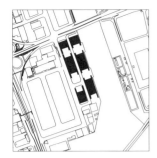

機能＝冷凍倉庫＋オフィス＋駐車場
場所＝大田区平和島
京浜運河とモノレールに挟まれて9棟ならぶ巨大冷凍倉庫○荷下ろし用のプラットフォームと事務所が駐車場を囲み，背後に巨大冷凍倉庫○コンクリートの厚い壁にあけられたテーパーつきの窓はスイスの山岳住居風○クーリングタワーの音がＢＧＭ○都市の冷蔵庫

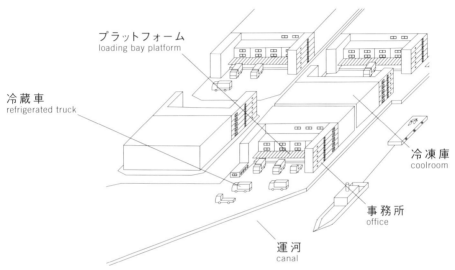

プラットフォーム
loading bay platform

冷蔵車
refrigerated truck

冷凍庫
coolroom

事務所
office

運河
canal

62
ＴＲＤ（東京冷凍団地）冷凍団地ビル
coolroom estate

function: coolroom storage units + office + truck parking
site: Heiwa-jima, Ota-ku
- sandwiched between the Keihin canal and
the monorail is a line of nine enormous coolroom units
- offices and the truck loading platform enclose a parking area
- the thick concrete walls of the coolroom are punctured with openings tapering
to small windows in the style of the traditional Swiss cottage
- background music of the refrigeration radiator units
- refrigerator for the city

機能＝自動販売機＋オフィス
場所＝品川区大崎
狭小な敷地に建つべくして建てられた小さな建物◯自動
販売機で武装◯類例多数

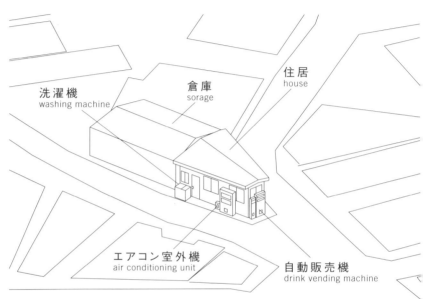

洗濯機
washing machine

倉庫
sorage

住居
house

エアコン室外機
air conditioning unit

自動販売機
drink vending machine

63
ペット建築1号
pet architecture 001

function: house + drink machine
site: Osaki, Shinagawa-ku
- a single storey house on a tiny triangular site
- a small landmark within an industrial area
- armed with drink machines to two sides and the tip
- there are many other examples of this phenomenon

機能＝調整池＋公園＋マンション
場所＝中野区松が丘,新宿区西落合
妙正寺川の調整池の上に集合住宅○建築と河川工学の
混血○足元はふだんは公園だが増水時には水没する○雨
降りのパターンに敏感に反応する都市居住の形式○壁打
ちテニス場あり

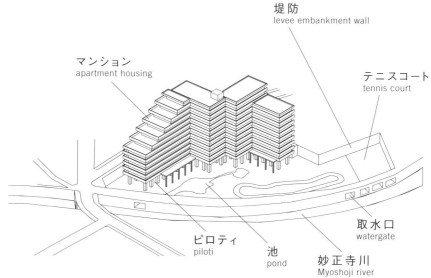

マンション
apartment housing

堤防
levee embankment wall

テニスコート
tennis court

ピロティ
piloti

池
pond

妙正寺川
Myoshoji river

取水口
watergate

64
ダムマンション
dam housing

function: reservoir + park + apartments
site: Matsugaoka, Nakano-ku, also Nishi-ochiai, Shinjuku-ku
- apartment buildings over reservoir for Myoshoji river
- the base of the apartment buildings are a park at normal times,
automatically converting into a reservoir at times of heavy rainfall
- urban living can still retain a high consciousness of natural rainfall patterns
- the tennis wall can be converted to a new game of water tennis
- a confluence of architecture and river engineering

機能＝空港ターミナル
場所＝中央区日本橋蛎殻町，箱崎町
東京の空港ターミナル○浜町ランプ脇，首都高6号線と
9号線のジャンクションの下の400mのビル○首都高か
ら分岐する道路が建物に貫通○ある意味ステルス的建
築でヴォリュームとして捉えがたい

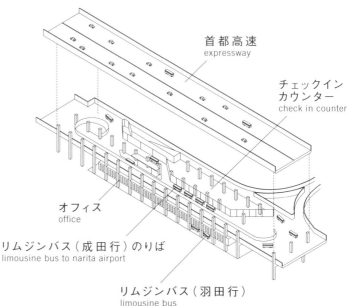

首都高速
expressway

チェックイン
カウンター
check in counter

オフィス
office

リムジンバス（成田行）のりば
limousine bus to narita airport

リムジンバス（羽田行）
limousine bus

65
ジャンクションターミナル
airport junction

function: airport terminal
site: Hakozaki-cho, Chuo-ku
- inner city airport terminal
- 400 metre long building under the junction of
expressway no.6 and no.9 and beside the Hamacho exit
- sections of the main expressway route and
branches penetrate this building at mid level
- a kind of 'stealth' architecture,
whose volume is almost imperceivable

機能＝テニスコート＋首都高トンネル
場所＝渋谷区渋谷
青山学院のグラウンドのまん中○首都高速と六本木通り
にうかんだテニスコート○夜はネットが光る○まさに都市
のテニス○排気ガスに注意

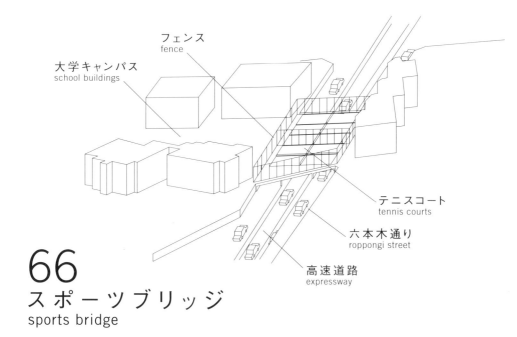

大学キャンパス
school buildings

フェンス
fence

テニスコート
tennis courts

六本木通り
roppongi street

高速道路
expressway

66
スポーツブリッジ
sports bridge

function: tennis court + expressway tunnel
site: Shibuya, Shibuya-ku
- courts on the rooftop of Aoyama tunnel,
over Roppongi street and the metropolitan expressway
- tennis courts on the premises of Aoyama Gakuin private school
- the courts are next to the sports ground,
which is central to the primary, middle and high schools
- possibility of playing tennis whilst watching the stream of cars below

機能＝ゴルフ練習場＋テニスコート
＋クラブハウス＋集合住宅
場所＝目黒区上目黒
林の中に挿入されたスポーツ用の檻の複合○自然の斜面を
利用してボールを回収するゴルフ打放しがはじまり○斜面の
下から上に向けて打つとボールが斜面を転がって戻ってくる
○クラブハウスには喫茶店や更衣室だけでなくパターゴルフ
場も入っている○人間が檻の中で色々なスポーツをしてい
る様は、まるでヒト科の動物園

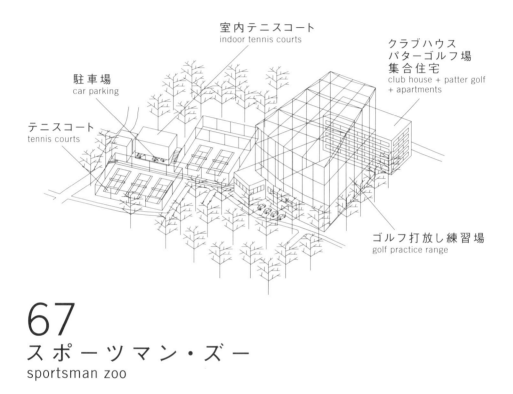

室内テニスコート
indoor tennis courts

クラブハウス
パターゴルフ場
集合住宅
club house + patter golf
+ apartments

駐車場
car parking

テニスコート
tennis courts

ゴルフ打放し練習場
golf practice range

67
スポーツマン・ズー
sportsman zoo

function: golf practice range + tennis courts + club house
site: Kami-meguro, Meguro-ku
- a gathering of sports cages in the woods
- the golf range utilises the slope of the land for the ball return
- the club house does not only include a cafe
and changing rooms, but also an indoor patter golf course
- the vision of humans playing various sports
in these cages is just like going to the zoo

機能＝倉庫＋オフィスビル＋ヘリポート＋看板
場所＝港区海岸
港湾通りと運河に挟まれた細い敷地。高速道路やモノレールが近くを走る○陸海空から使える倉庫とオフィスビルの屋上をヘリポートで連結○ヘリポートの基壇は看板になっている○３０分置きに飛び立つヘリコプター。日曜日定休○周辺にはレインボーブリッジ，お台場など，湾岸のシンボルが多い

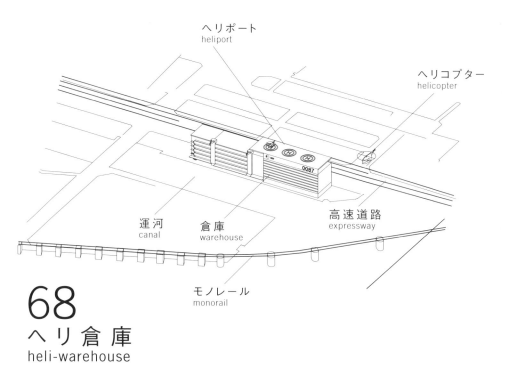

ヘリポート
heliport

ヘリコプター
helicopter

運河
canal

倉庫
warehouse

高速道路
expressway

モノレール
monorail

68
ヘリ倉庫
heli-warehouse

function: heliport + warehouse + billboard
site: Kaigan, Minato-ku
- a narrow site sandwiched between the bayside road
and a canal with an expressway to the side
- the warehouse can be accessed from land, sea and sky
- the crowning ring of billboards becomes the podium for the heliport
- helicopters come over every half hour, interacting with
the bayside symbols of rainbow bridge, ferry terminal, and Odaiba

機能＝洗車場
場所＝渋谷区代々木
山手通り拡幅の副産物。都市計画道路予定地内の時
限付き施設○メタリックでマシニックだけどおもちゃっぽ
い外観○2階の手洗車か1階の機械洗車か入口で選択
○機械洗車はドライブスルー○機械と人間が上下階に
重なって洗車のうまさを競い合っている

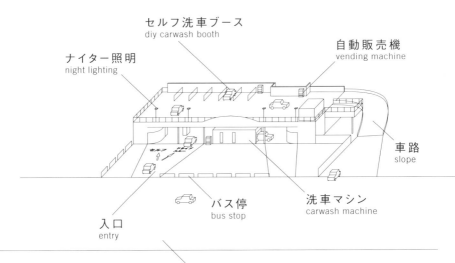

セルフ洗車ブース
diy carwash booth

自動販売機
vending machine

ナイター照明
night lighting

車路
slope

洗車マシン
carwash machine

バス停
bus stop

入口
entry

山手通り
Yamate street

69
洗 車 テ ラ ス
carwash terrace

function: diy carwash + machine carwash
site: Yoyogi, Shibuya-ku
- temporary facility utilising land set aside
for future widening of Yamate street
- metallic and machinistic, yet toy like appearance
- the machine carwash is drive through
- at the entry point, drivers select from upper level
diy carwash and ground level machine wash
- can your skills and speed compete with the machine?

機能＝射撃練習場＋墓地
場所＝新座市新塚
遺跡跡地利用。東京オリンピックの射撃競技場だった○土手で囲われた内部は現在、自衛隊敷地内の射撃練習場○墓から射撃は見えないが射撃音あり○銃と墓場の隣接。よく考えれば背筋が凍る

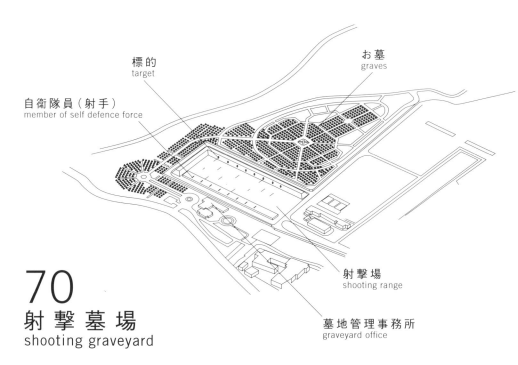

標的
target

お墓
graves

自衛隊員（射手）
member of self defence force

射撃場
shooting range

墓地管理事務所
graveyard office

70
射 撃 墓 場
shooting graveyard

function: shooting range + graveyard
site: Niizuka, Niiza-shi
- site for the Tokyo Olympic shooting range,
utilising the grounds of an ancient tomb
- now it is used for practice by the self defence forces
- it is hidden by surrounding embankments,
but the sound of shooting is very near
- the adjacency of guns and graveyard: a chilling thought

M A P
地図

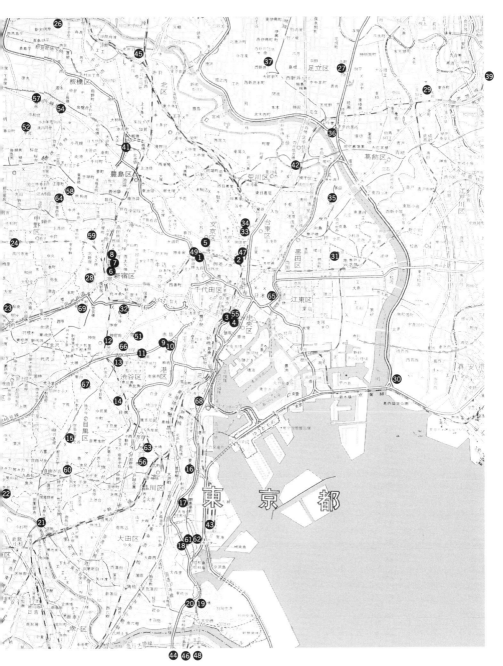

TALK WITH TAKASHI HOMMA
ホンマタカシとの対話

2000年5月7日　ホンマタカシ（TH）×貝島桃代（MK）＋黒田潤三（K）＋塚本由晴（YT）
TH: Takashi Homma × MK: Momoyo Kaijima ＋ K: Junzo Kuroda ＋ YT: Yoshiharu Tsukamoto　May 7 , 2000

「がははおもしれえ」

MK○まずはじめに、東京で活動している建築家としては、東京で写真家として活動しているホンマさんが「メイド・イン・トーキョー」をどうみてるのか、聞いてみたいところです。

TH○赤瀬川源平の超芸術トマソンとはどう違うって公式には言ってるんでしたっけ？

MK○トマソンは、まちを歩くことで探しだした都市の記憶の断片から現実の都市空間のうえに、無数の小さな歴史を物語ろうとする試みですよね。だからどこかノスタルジックで、過去は振り返れるんだけど、未来は描きにくい感じがある。実際に東京で建物を作ろうとするときの展開としてはむずかしい。でも自分たちには今の都市がどう使えるかが重要だし、その未来へのパースペクティブを描きたかったんです。

TH○なるほど、ノスタルジーではないということですね。じゃあ、メイド・イン・トーキョーの建物をよく「ダメ」って言ってますが、どうしてそこに興味をもったんですか？

MK○これらの建物は、いわゆる建築作品の常識からすると「ダメ」なんだけど、良くみるとすごく面白い。だから否定じゃなくて愛すべきものとしての「ダメ」。

YT○生真面目過ぎて、逆に現実のカリカチュアになっちゃった建物も多いんです。真剣にやってると、どこかユーモラスにみえてくる感じとか、都市の中での「オフ」な感覚とか。

TH○メイド・イン・トーキョーには、東京が結構緊張してるなかでの「がははおもしれえ」ってものを感じるんですよ。

MK○その感じは狙ってます。東京みたいに高密度で混乱した都市に、シリアスな戦いを挑むのはつらいから（笑）。

TH○「がははおもしろい」っていうパワーは結構重要じゃないかと思う。あのセメント工場のやつ（「生コンアパート」）なんて、ばかばかしくていい。「エレクトリックパッサージュ」とか、名前のつけ方も最高にうまいよね。

フラット

TH○写真といっしょに、線画の絵を描いているじゃないですか。あれは予想で描いているんですか？

JK○自分たちの解釈は入ってます。コンピューターで描いたおかげで、手分けして描いたけど各自の個性が出ないようになった。それと、仕上げとか光の感じとかをレンダリングして現実に近づけるんじゃなくて、内部を透かしたりして見せたい所を強調しています。

TH○僕が最初にかっこいいなとおもったのが写真よりもドローイングですよね。写真と地図や解説だけだったら普通だし、おそらくよく分からない。でもこのドローイングまでくるとぐっとくる（笑）。

MK○それはホンマさんが写真家だから？（笑）。

TH○というか…なんかドローイングの方が、平面的にみれるんだよね。

YT○ああいう建物を、意味を問わない状態でフラットに見

TH○ The buildings of Made in Tokyo are often described as 'no good' (da-me). Why is it that you started to become interested in this quality?

MK○ These buildings are regarded as da-me from the point of view of architectural magazines, but if you look closely at them they are very interesting. So, this da-me is not only negative, but also adorable.

YT○ They are too serious - in fact many of them have become a caricature of their urban reality. Their da-me includes humour pouring out of their ridiculous seriousness, and release from the city.

TH○ Made in Tokyo seems to let me laugh freely, while in amongst the tension of Tokyo.

MK○ We are after exactly that feeling. After all, trying to pick a fight with the high density and confusion of Tokyo is pretty hard. (laughter)

TH○ At the beginning, I thought the drawings were a lot cooler than the photos. If it was only the photos, maps and explanations, it would be quite normal, and actually fairly hard to understand. But when I get to the drawings, it really hits me.

MK○ Is that because you are a photographer?

TH○ Well, in fact I seem to be able to see more surface plane in the drawings.

YT○ When we tried to look at the buildings as flatly and without value judgements as possible, they became black and white line drawings. With a photo, you can't keep out the nuances of neon colours, urban grime etc.

ることを徹底させたら白黒の線画になった。写真だとやっぱりネオンの色とか、汚れとか、ニュアンスが写ったりしますから。

TH○そうですよね。「ゴルフタクシービル」を僕が撮ったときにも思ったんですけど、写真だと余計な物までいろいろ入っちゃうから困るなあと。ドローイングだと、余計な物は排除できるところがいいですよね。

アホ・ドローイング

MK○それに、なるべく可愛くなるように描いてます。車とか建物のまわりにあるものを書き込むのも大事。そうすることで建物と周囲の関係がみえてくる。

JK○細かくミキサー車まで描くと全然違うんですよ。この馬もふつうよりちょっと大きいんですけどね。競走馬のプロポーションじゃない(笑)。

TH○建物の比率はあってるんですか？

JK○プロポーションは変えてます。大きな建物とか平べったくなっちゃうからデフォルメして。

YT○建物をみつけて写真をとって線で描く。あのドローイングを描くのにもけっこう手がかかるし、センスというか訓練が必要です。線はどれも同じ太さで、情感とかなくしていく。するとそれぞれの建物から引きをとっているけど、実は愛情がこもってる状態が訪れます。

TH　素人に写真見せて、「これってバス団地なんだよ、すご

いだろ！」っていってもわかんないだろうけど、ドローイングまできて「ああ、そうなんだって」わかる。つまりドローイングによって、はじめて見方が語られる気がしますね。

MK　それを藤森さんたちは言葉でやってたんだと思う。

JK　よく歴史の人たちにはもっと語れっていわれます。

TH　いや、これを物語みたいにして語ったら最悪ですよ。

MK　未来があるようにと、目の前にあるままを書くことに徹したら、こういう風にシンプルになった。

YT　写真だけだと時には批判にもみえちゃうんだよね。「こんな建物でいいのか！」っていうような。

TH　社会問題とかね。某週刊誌によくあるよね。

MK　メイド・イン・トーキョーも都市の現状に対する批判と思われてしまうところがあります...。ホンマさんの「TOKYO SUBURBIA」も、そういわれませんでした？

TH　実際、あれを批判だと捉えてる大人は多いよね。

YT　でもこのドローイングだと批判にはみえなくなると思うんだけど。アホ・ドローイングっていうか、イノセントっていうか、カーンと抜けるっていうか...。

TH　すごく良いですよ、ここで突き抜ける感じ。ドローイングはめちゃくちゃ重要だと思いますよ。

批判であることを越えて

YT　生コンアパートにホンマさんを連れてったんだけど、「うーん」て唸って結局撮らなかったのは印象的でした。

TH: I think that for an everyday person, it is the drawings that make clear what is so exciting about the photos.
MK○ It is what Fujimori-san was trying to do in words. (Terunobu Fujimori et al, Institute of Street Observation)
JK○ Often, historians say to us that we should put it more into words.
TH○ Oh no! If you turn it into a story, that will be the end.
MK○ It has become practical, because we simply concentrated on describing what was in front of us, and we wanted to leave room for the future.
YT○ If there are only photos, then they can be taken as just criticism. Like 'is this building really ok?' But I think that by making the drawings, it can't be seen as purely critical any more. These drawings are foolish, innocent, speedy . . .

TH: I think the way the work passes right through the criticism is really good. The drawings are hugely important.
YT: It was very memorable for me that when we went together to the nama-con apartment house, you didn't take any photos. You said 'hmm – it just doesn't give joy without the drawings and text.'
TH: Rather than the building itself, the interest is guided by the drawings of 'Made in Tokyo'.
MK: The Tokyo which we see, and the Tokyo which you see, are different aren't they. When I saw your works of 'TOKYO SUBURBIA', on the one hand I thought 'oh, this is entirely different from Made in Tokyo', but then on the other hand, I thought 'yes, I can understand this.' I think it is interesting that we want to see different aspects of the same Tokyo.

「やっぱり絵とか解説とかないとおもしろくないなあ」って（笑）。

TH　実際の建物より、説明ドローイングがついて、「メイド・イン・トーキョー」というガイドブックを通してあらためてみると、ぜん面白いんですよ。(笑)

MK　私たちのみてる東京とホンマさんのみてる東京は違いますよね。わたしもホンマさんの「TOKYO SUBURBIA」をみて「あっ、メイド・イン・トーキョーとは全然違う」と思ったと同時に「ああ、なるほどな」って思いました。同じ東京を切り取っても別の所みたい。それが面白いなあと思う。

TH　ほら、荒木さんとか篠山さんとかも、「おれが東京をとる」って言ってるし、建築家にもいるでしょう。でも東京にはいろんな見方がある。ひとりの人で撮りきれるものじゃないよ。だから僕の見方とメイド・イン・トーキョーが違うのは当然ですよね。「TOKYO SUBURBIA」でも「あれが郊外のすべてだなんて認めない」っていう批判をよく言われるけど、全然僕は「これが東京の郊外だ！」なんて言い切ってないんですよ。あくまでイチ断面ですから。でも物件が70もあるとかっこいいですよね。しかもそれを使ったり住んだりしてる人が何も知らないってことが楽しいですね。

軽い都市論

MK　コルビュジエとか、ふつう建築家はもっと都市の全体をみたいって言うじゃない？それが都市論の正道かもしれないけど、それは我々にとってはリアルじゃない。ある個人がみた東京がすべてだなんてとても言えないぐらい、東京は大きいと思うから。だからメイド・イン・トーキョーは都市論としてはすごく軽いっていうか、正道じゃないかもしれないけど、それだから具体的に都市を捉えることができる可能性があるように思う。

TH　ていうか東京には、むしろそれぐらいでいてもらいたいよね。だれかひとりの人に語り尽くされちゃったら、面白くない。やっぱり東京論とかっていうのは傲慢だよ。せっかく東京でやってるんだから、東京にはもっと巨大なものであってもらいたいんだよね。だれかにまとめられちゃったら、そこでやる意味がないし、ばかばかしいじゃない。それに東京はそんなに簡単なものじゃないと思うんだよね。

「メイド・イン・トーキョー」にしても「TOKYO SUBURBIA」にしても、イラだつ人たちがいるとすると、その言い分は、これは批判なのかそれとも賛美なのかはっきりしてくれってことだと思うけど。

MK　はっきりしないほうがいいと思うんだよね。

TH　はっきりさせられないんだよ。そんな簡単じゃないですよね。

JK　はじめの展覧会の時に建築学会の事務局の人も「ダメ建築」っていう言い方を結構心配してました。問題になったらどうするんですか？って。

YT　でも意外にそういう苦情はこないね。

TH: If anything, I hope Tokyo can sustain at least that much. It wouldn't be interesting if just one single person was able to completely explain everything. Since this is where we are working, I'd like Tokyo to be gargantuan! If someone explains the whole city, it becomes meaningless and stupid to work here. Anyway, I think Tokyo just isn't such a simple thing. Whether looking at 'Made in Tokyo' or 'TOKYO SUBURBIA', people who are irritated by our work are ones who want a definite position to be stated – are we being critical or appreciative?

MK: I think it's better to not be definite.

TH: More than anything, I feel that 'Made in Tokyo' is enjoying Tokyo. It is useless to criticise and go all dark and narcissistic, saying that the olden days were so much better.

People usually like the past. Even in photography, there is a tendency towards the nostalgia of sepia toned images, and critics often pick up on these. I do think that because everybody likes them, there is a high demand and so they are necessary. But if you aren't going to get appreciated, a different method of expression can be fruitless and tiring. It seems that photography is of the past after all. In terms of fact, it can only take images of the past. People become satisfied with nostalgia. But if that's all, I think photography has no future. I get annoyed by the way that critics don't seem to realise this.

YT: But, isn't it possible to look forwards, depending on what you fix into the image?

MK: In the collection of 'Made in Tokyo', some of the

MK　この本が出たら結構、たくさんきたりして！

TH　いいんじゃないですかクレームがあるくらいが。

MK　都市的な環境でやっているんだから、クレームは都市との関わりが多いことの証しかも？

TH　何より「メイド・イン・トーキョー」は、東京を楽しんでるって感じがするよね。やっぱり無理矢理ねじ伏せるとかはよくないですよ（笑）。批判して、暗くナルシスティックに昔はよかったなんて言ってもどうしようもないし。

東京の未来を写す？

MK　古い街並みのむこうに新宿の超高層がみえる写真とか、ああいう東京に対する見方って我々と何が違うのかな？

TH　人はやっぱり昔が好きだよね、写真にしても結局、昔に回帰してる。セピアっぽい色がすごくノスタルジックにみえて、評論家とかもそれを評価する傾向がある。みんな好きだから需要もあるし、必然性があるのかなって思っちゃうんだけど。新しい表現してもあんまり誉められないなら結構不毛だし、疲れるっていうか…（笑）。やっぱり写真って過去のものなんだよね。過去のものしか写せない。だから過去の懐かしさをみんな良しとするわけですよ。でもそればかりだと写真ってこれから行き詰まると思う。そのことにどうして評論家は気がつかないんだろうってイライラするんだよね。

YT　でも定着させるものの種類によっては、前向きにすることも可能でしょう？

MK　メイド・イン・トーキョーの建物とかでも、すでになくなっちゃった建物もある。保存運動しないの？って誰かに言われたけど、それもリアリティがないなって思う。

TH　そんなのは反対運動なしで壊して、さらにすごいピカピカのをつくった方がいいんじゃないですか（笑）。

MK　それぞれの建物が、いまの東京の状況をレポートしているものだとすれば、その役目がなくなったんならそれはそれでいいんじゃないかって。これらの建物の前向きな感じっていうか、捨て身な感じ、とにかく今を生きてる感じがすごくおもしろいから。

YT　その感じを写真に定着させることには未来があるような気がするな。

TH　でもこういった感覚って少数派ですよね。こんなことやっても理解されないかって思いつつやる。僕や塚本さんなんかはいつもどこかそういう自虐的な所がある。でも貝島さんはその狭いところをみんながわかってくれると思ってるんだよね。貝島さんのそういうところ、すごくおもしろいし、それは僕らにとっての希望でもある。僕が言ってダメでも、貝島さんが言うとみんなああそうかって（笑笑笑）。

MK　…。ところでこの本売れますかね？

TH　いやー、どうでしょう。

MK　それって売れないってことですか？

TH　売れればいいなーってことですよ。（笑笑笑）。

---

buildings have already been demolished. Someone asked me 'why don't you start up a preservation society?', but I think there is no reality in this.

TH: Isn't it better to demolish and rebuild a shiney-new, much more fantastic version? (laughter)

MK: If we understand each building as a measure of the current condition of Tokyo, surely it's ok for it to disappear once this role has become redundant. I am interested in the forward looking quality, the throw away feeling, in any case really-living-right-now sense of these buildings.

YT: I feel that there is a future in capturing those feelings through photography.

TH: But I think this way of thinking is in a minority. I keep doing it, even though I'm not sure if it is understood. But I think that Kaijima-san believes that everyone can understand. That aspect of Kaijima-san is very delightful, and I think it gives hope to the rest of us.

MK: . . . Mmm - anyway, do you think this book will sell? (laughter)

HISTORY
沿革

1991　渋谷にメイド・イン・トーキョー幻の第一号（バッティングセンター＋スパゲッティレストラン、数年後に取り壊される）を貝島・塚本が発見。その後数年間にわたり、「ゴルフタクシービル」「生コンアパート」などを発見。
The first "Made in Tokyo" building discovered in Shibuya by Kaijima+Tsukamoto. Several more candidates found over the following years.

1996　アーキテクチャー・オブ・ザ・イヤー1996「革命の建築博物館」展（磯崎新プロデュース）にて現代日本建築史のインスタレーションとして行われることが決定。
"Made in Tokyo" invited to take part as the contemporary history component of the exhibition "Architecture of the year 1996: architectural Museum of Revolution".

05　黒田、藤岡などと共にT.M.I.Tを組織。
T.M.I.T established with Kuroda and Fujioka.

09　イタリア、フィレンツェにてメイド・イン・トーキョーをめぐり、貝島が展覧会プロデューサー磯崎新と対話。
（展覧会カタログ『磯崎新の革命遊戯』（TOTO出版）にメイド・イン・トーキョー30物件の紹介とともに収録）
Discussion on the run in Florence, Kaijima and Arata Isozaki about the publication of Made in Tokyo for the exhibition catalogue.

11　展覧会。メイド・イン・トーキョーの建物をプリントした300枚のTシャツを制作流通させるインスタレーションが行われた。
Exihibition installation including 300 T-shirts.

1997　03,04　「10+1 vol.8」「intercommunication vol.20」にて紹介
Publication in "10+1" vol.8 and "intercommunication", vol.20.

04　東京工業大学大学院塚本ゼミナールにてさらに調査が進められる
Development by the master course student class in Tokyo Institute of Technology

07　貝島、「メイド・イン・ホンコン」をSD7月号に発表
Made in Hongkong is published in "Space Design" 1997 July. Kaijima Institute Publishing.

09　スイス・チューリッヒ、アーキテクチュア・フォーラムにて初の海外個展
Exhibition in Architektur Forum Zurich.

1998　06　メイド・イン・トーキョー　インターネット日本語版完成
http://www.dnp.co.jp/museum/nmp/madeintokyo/mit.html
Japanese version web site was opened

12　ホンマタカシ「TOKYO SUBURBIA」展模型
"New Suburbia Made in Tokyo"（於：パルコギャラリー）
Model "New Suburbia Made in Tokyo" . Collaboration with Takashi Homma for the exhibition at Parco Gallery

1999　02　第11回「近代、都市・建築」研究会にて森川氏、後藤氏とパネルディスカッション（貝島）（於：東京大学）
Panel disscusion between Kaijima and Kaichiro Morikawa, Takeshi Goto in Studies of "Modernity / Urbanism / Architecture "

05　21世紀学生会議「トーキョー・リサイクル・ガイドブック」
Tokyo Recycle Guide Book in 21st Century Students Conference

11　メイド・イン・トーキョー　インターネット英語版完成、ヴェネツィアビエンナーレ　ウェブ展出品
http://www.dnp.co.jp/museum/nmp/madeintokyo_e/mit.html
English version web site was opened. Invitation to "Expo on line" of Venice Biennale

2001　02　バルセロナにてワークショップ・講演・展覧会
Workshop, lecture and exhibition in limits col. legi.d' Arqhitectes de Catalunya, Barcelona

PROFILE
略 歴

貝島桃代 かいじまももよ

1969年、東京都生まれ。1991年、日本女子大学
住居学科卒。1992年、塚本由晴とアトリエ・ワン設
立。1994年、東京工業大学大学院修士過程修了。
1996年、スイス連邦工科大学奨学生。2000年、
東京工業大学大学院博士課程満期退学。現在、
筑波大学専任講師。
主な作品はすべて塚本と共同で、「ミニ・ハウス」
（1999年 平成11年度東京建築士会住宅建築賞
金賞／2000年新建築吉岡賞）、「川西町営コテー
ジB」（1999年）、「モカハウス」（2000年）、「ハウ
ス アサマ」（2001年）など。主な著書は、「特集都
市に向かう透明性 スイス・ドイツ語圏の建築」（監
修、『SD』9802）、「トーキョー・リサイクル計画
10+1 no.21」（共著、2000年、INAX出版）、「も
っと小さな家」（2001年、アトリエ・ワン出版）、「ペ
ット・アーキテクチャー・ガイドブック」（2001年、ワ
ールド・フォト・プレス）など。

黒田潤三 くろだじゅんぞう

1968年に茨城県生まれ。1992年武蔵野美術大学
造形学部建築学科卒。1992年―96年東京工業
大学坂本一成研究室研究生。1996年より個人に
て美術、建築活動開始。
主な作品は「ウォッシュマン」（1995年）、「森の戸
建住宅」（1996年近未来戸建住宅デザインコンペ
ティション最優秀賞）「ソフトハウス」（1998年フィ
リップ・モリス・アートアワード入選）、「タナダパーク」
（2000年妻有アートトリエンナーレ公募展入選）など。

塚本由晴 つかもとよしはる

1965年、神奈川県生まれ。1987年、東京工業大
学工学部建築学科卒。1987-88年、UP8（パリ）
自由聴講生。1992年、貝島桃代とアトリエ・ワン設立。
1994年東京工業大学大学院博士課程修了。現
在 同大学大学院助教授,博士（工学）。
主な作品は貝島の項参照。主な著書は、「ハウジン
グ・プロジェクト・トウキョウ」（共著、東海大学出版
1998年）「トーキョー・リサイクル計画10+1 no.21」
（共著、2000年、INAX出版）、「もっと小さな家」（2001
年、アトリエ・ワン出版）、「ペット・アーキテクチャー・ガ
イドブック」（2001年、ワールド・フォト・プレス）など。

Momoyo Kaijima

1969 Born in Tokyo. 1991 Graduated from
Department of Housing, Faculty of Home Economics,
Japan Women's University. 1992 Established Atelier
Bow-wow with Yoshiharu Tsukamoto. 1994
Completed the Master Course of Architecture, Tokyo
Institute of Technology. 1996-97 Studied at the
Federal Institute of Technology (ETH), Zurich. 2000
Completed the Doctor Course, Tokyo Institute of
Technology. Currently assistant professor at Faculty
of art, Tsukuba University. Main works; "mini-
house,1999 " "Kawanishi camping cottageB, 1999"
"mocahouse,2000" "houses asama,2001" etc. Main
books "Architecture of Swiss german, SD9802"
"Tokyo Recycle Projects 10+1 no.21 INAX
Publishing" "LES PLUS PETITES MAISONS",2001,
Atelier Bow-wow publishing "Pet Architecture Guide
book",2001,World photo press etc.

Junzo Kuroda

1968 Born in Ibaraki Prefecture. 1992 Graduated
from Department of Architecture at Musashino Art
University. 1992-96 Studied as a research student
at the Sakamoto Laboratory of Tokyo Institute of
Technology. 1996 Started as a freelance architect
and artist. Main works; "WASHMAN" "House of a
forest" "Soft house" "Tanada Park" etc.

Yoshiharu Tsukamoto

1965 Born in Kanagawa Prefecture. 1987
Graduated from Department of Architecture and
Building Engineering, Faculty of Engineering, Tokyo
Institute of Technology. 1987-88 Studied at Ecole
d'Architecture de Paris- Bellevile. 1992 Established
Atelier Bow-wow with Momoyo Kaijima.1994
Completed the Doctor Course, Tokyo Institute of
Technology. Currently associate professor at
Department of Architecture and Building
Engineering, Faculty of Engineering, Tokyo Institute
of Technology, and Doctor of Engineering. Main
works see the list of Kaijima. Main books "Housing
Project Tokyo,1998" "Tokyo Recycle Projects 10+1
no.21 INAX Publishing, 2000" "LES PLUS PETITES
MAISONS", 2001, Atelier Bow-wow publishing "Pet
Architecture Guide book",2001,World photo press
etc.

BIBLIOGRAPHY

書誌

1996/12/10 『磯崎新の革命遊戯』p.223-280 TOTO出版 [1]
　　　　　　「ダメ建築礼賛」p.249-271
　　　　　　「メイド・イン・トーキョー」p.249-271
　　　　　　「空白恐怖症の東京」p.272-280
　　　　　　Arata Isozaki's Revolution Game p.223-280, TOTO Publishers.
　　　　　　Dame-Architecture p.249-271
　　　　　　made in tokyo p.249-271
　　　　　　Void-Fear in Tokyo p.272-280

1997/01 　　『新建築』9701／p.195-198 [2]
　　　　　　特別記事:96アーキテクチュア・オブ・ザ・イヤー批評
　　　　　　「カメラ・オブスキュラあるいは革命の建築博物館」展
　　　　　　すなわち磯崎新のエンドレス・デスマッチ　土居義岳
　　　　　　Shinkenchiku 9701 p.195-198
　　　　　　Architectural Museum of Revolution Exhibition
　　　　　　or Arata Isozaki's Endless Mach by Yoshitake Dohi

1997/02 　　『建築文化』vol.52／no.604／1997.2／p.10 [3]
　　　　　　「建築史とのつきあい方」橋本憲一郎
　　　　　　Kenchikubunka vol.52 no.604 1997, 2 p.10
　　　　　　How to play with Architecture History by Kenichiro Hashimoto

1997/04/01 『Inter Communication』20／p.8-9／NTT出版 [4]
　　　　　　『都市の未来形型』メイド・イン・トーキョー
　　　　　　Inter Communication 20 p.8-9 NTT publishing
　　　　　　The Shape of Cities in the Future [I]

1998/02/10 『10＋1』No.12／p.80-90／INAX出版 [5]
　　　　　　「他者が欲望する黒船都市,トーキョー」五十嵐太郎
　　　　　　10+1" No.12, p.80-90, INAX
　　　　　　Delirious blackship city, Tokyo by Taro Igarashi

1998/04/01 『SD』9804／p.52／アトリエ・ワン Recent Works／鹿島出版会 [6]
　　　　　　SD 9804 p.52 Atelier Bow-wow Recent Works Kajima Publishing

1998/07/25 『A』1998 vol.1／PULP CITY／p.20-21 [7]
　　　　　　「メイド・イン・トーキョー」＝New Urban Architecture Style
　　　　　　A 1998 vol.1, PULP CITY, p.20-21
　　　　　　Made in Tokyo=New Urban Architecture Style

1998/07/30 『山形新聞』7面,うえーぶ98「東京の"ダメ建築"集める」[8]
　　　　　　Yamagata Shinbun P7 WAVE 98
　　　　　　"Collecting Dame-Architecture in Tokyo"

1998/08/24 『日経アーキテクチュア』p.102-105／日経BP社 [9]
　　　　　　「都市の再発見 City Observation」
　　　　　　Nikkei Architecture p.102-105 Nikkei BP
　　　　　　"Re-discovering the City: City Observation"

発行―――2001年8月20日 第1刷ⓒ 2004年12月30日 第6刷
著者―――貝島桃代十黒田潤三十塚本由晴
写真―――ホンマタカシ（表紙・見返し・P6-7・P40-41）
　　　　　金町自動車教習所（P99）
　　　　　チーム・メイド・イン・トーキョー
デザイン――古平正義
発行者―――鹿島光一
発行所―――鹿島出版会
　　　　　〒107-8345 東京都港区赤坂6丁目5番13号
　　　　　電話03-5561-2550 振替00160-2-180883
印刷―――壮光舎印刷
製本―――富士製本

メイド・イン・トーキョー
MADE IN TOKYO

First Published in Japan, 20 August, 2001
by Kajima Institute Publishing Co., Ltd.

6-5-13 Akasaka, Minato-ku, Tokyo 107-8345 Japan
tel. 03-5561-2550

Authors: Momoyo Kaijima
　　　　 Junzo Kuroda
　　　　 Yoshiharu Tsukamoto
Photographers: Takashi Homma (cover, endpaper, P6-7, P40-41)
　　　　　　　　 Kanamachi Driving School (P99)
　　　　　　　　 Team Made in Tokyo
Design: Masayoshi Kodaira
Publisher: Kinya Arai

Printed in Japan

ISBN4-306-04421-1 C3052
本書の内容に関するご意見・ご感想は下記までお寄せ下さい。
URL：http//：www.kajima-publishing.co.jp
E-mail：info@kajima-publishing.co.jp